# THE SIX BRIDES OF DILSTON

# THE SIX BRIDES OF DILSTON

## A.R.C. BOLTON

NEW HORIZON

ISBN 0 7125 0008 1 √

Published and printed by
NEW HORIZON (Transeuros Limited)
BOGNOR REGIS
GREAT BRITAIN

# FOREWORD

By Dorothy Middleton, author of Victorian
Lady Travellers, Routledge & Kegan Paul.

The feminist movements of our day have
stimulated interest in the position of
women in past times, and Rollo Bolton's
*The Six Brides of Dilston* offers an
unusually complete picture of the distaff
side of a Victorian family. This is to be
welcomed, because while studies of
outstanding individual women – writers,
artists, social reformers, travellers – are
not wanting, the domestic scene is often
treated as no more than a background.
Primarily, of course, we have here a
work of family piety, commemorating the
author's grandmother, born Emily Grey,
and her five sisters, all of whom left
their own record in the form of letters or
published works. But Mr. Bolton has not
contented himself with a static
description of domestic life; he has
sought also to relate it to what was
going on in the world and how it
affected the women of the family. His
'brides' were the daughters of John Grey
(1785–1868), a notable Northumbrian
landowner and agriculturist who was
involved in many of the important
political and social movements of his
day, in particular the anti–slavery
crusade. He was appointed in 1833 to
administer property in Northumberland
and Cumberland belonging to Greenwich
Hospital, including estates, once the

property of the ill-fated Radcliffe family, which were sequestrated after the failure of the Jacobite rising of 1715. John Grey and his wife, born Hannah Eliza Annett, lived at Dilston near Corbridge where they raised their family of three sons and six daughters. Probably the best known of the Grey daughters is Josephine Butler, the social reformer, who has been the subject of biographies on which Mr. Bolton has some interesting comments to make. The reader will soon discover, however, that Josephine was not the only daughter to be involved in the trends and politics of the time, either at home or abroad. Harriet's marriage to the Swiss banker Tell Meuricoffre took her to live in Naples and introduced her to Garibaldi; Mary Ann's husband had fought for Greek independence in his youth; Emily's second husband was Lord Derby's agent in Ireland, and Eliza's husband a surgeon in Hong Kong. Josephine, helped from time to time by Fanny, was in the thick of the social reforms which were as much a feature of Victorian life as the abuses which resulted from the Industrial Revolution. Rollo Bolton is peculiarly well placed to record the doings of his forebears. A certain degree of inter-marriage between Greys, Boltons and Butlers has resulted in his access to many family papers, particularly those of his cousin, the late A.S.G. Butler, Josephine's grandson and biographer, and incidentally my own second cousin on the Butler side.

20 July 1982.

# CONTENTS PAGE

This concerns the six daughters of
John Grey, a Northumbrian landowner, agriculturist and administrator. The six girls born before
Queen Victoria's Coronation appropriately named Early Victorians.
Three principal topics pursued
against the background of contemporary society in Northumberland.
Namely: Parentage, Upbringing,
Married Lives.

Their grandparents and parents, all
Northumbrians. John Grey's school-
days. The family home at Milfield
Hill. John Grey assumes responsibility for management of the family
property. His marriage. His
professional contacts. His political
activities. His appointment as
Administrator of Greenwich Hospital
Estates. Political activities
debarred.

# CONTENTS

# AUTHOR'S NOTE and ACKNOWLEDGEMENTS

Ten years ago I completed, for private circulation, an account of the Bolton family from Northumberland and its connections. The account was based on family records and on material passed to me by my cousin, A.S.G. Butler, which he had used for his book, *Portrait of Josephine Butler*, published in 1954.

I could picture John Grey, my great grandfather, coping with his large family. To quote one of them: "He led his six daughters, each in turn, on her wedding-day, up the aisle of the village church, as years went on, and one by one, they quitted their father's home".

In September 1980 I visited Northumberland to look at places of interest to the family. Canon Chadwick showed me St. Andrew's Corbridge, the Parish Church, in the churchyard of which are the graves of John and Hannah Grey, and I was shown over Dilston Hall, where the Grey children were brought up. These two imposing edifices are today just as they were depicted in the 1840's in contemporary drawings.

Subsequently I recorded all that I knew, and was able to learn, about the six Grey girls, the youngest of whom was my grandmother Emily, and the present account is the outcome.

I acknowledge gratefully the help I have received from the following. Rev. Geoffrey Birtill, Minister, The Moravian Church House, London; Major Baker-

Creswell; Canon G.B. Chadwick, Vicar of St. Andrews, Corbridge for his welcome and help; Chester City Record Office. Mr. J.R. Daglish of Liverpool for research and a map; Mr. Robin M. Gard, County Archivist, Newcastle-upon-Tyne; Mr. G. Franklin Gray, Director, The Advanced Social Training Unit, Corbridge, located at Dilston Hall; Mrs B.L. Hough, Archivist at Church House, Westminster; Rev. T.G. Ridley; Mr. R.W.T. Thorp; Mr. L.P. Wenham, an authority on Richmond School; Father Joseph Williamson; Mr. A.G. Woodhead, the Keeper of the College Records, Corpus Christi College, Cambridge; Mr. W.L. St. Clair, Fellow of All Souls College, Oxford for the loan of an invaluable record.

I would also like to acknowledge the unstinting help given me by the Information Staff at Bourne Hall Library, Ewell.

All the typing involved in the preparation of my book in its various stages was done by my wife. Without her help I could not have achieved my goal.

# CHAPTER I

## INTRODUCTION

My father, Arthur William Bolton, died in 1912. I learnt from him about two men whom he much admired: his father, Jasper Bolton, and his maternal grandfather, John Grey. Subsequently, I learnt that John Grey's family comprised three sons and six daughters, of whom one was Josephine Butler and the youngest was Emily Bolton, my grandmother. In later life I got to know the late A.S.G. Butler, a distinguished architect, who was Josephine Butler's grandson and who wrote a book about her entitled *Portrait of Josephine Butler;* Faber & Faber, 1954.

The parents of Andrew Butler, as he was known in the family, were Stanley Butler and Rhoda Bolton, my father's eldest sister. Andrew passed to me certain items illustrating the somewhat involved family connections which are described in this work.

Josephine Butler wrote a book about her father, entitled *Memoir of John Grey of Dilston;* Henry S. King & Co, 1869, revised in 1875. It is a mine of information but is without an index and needs to be carefully combed by anyone looking for a clear picture of John Grey and his wife or of their numerous children individually.

In the several books which have been written about Josephine Butler and her

1

work as a social reformer, comparatively little attention has been paid to her parents or her brothers and sisters. The principal source available to the authors has been Josephine Butler's own book about her father. They have followed the general pattern of the book and did not grasp that John Grey's working life spanned exactly sixty years and that he became well-known in Northumberland as an agriculturist in two quite distinct capacities: first, as a landed proprietor and tenant farmer, who was also deeply involved in local politics, over a period of thirty years; and subsequently during a further thirty years, as the Receiver, or Administrator, of vast estates in Northumberland belonging to Greenwich Hospital. In this capacity participation by John Grey in party politics was expressly ruled out under the terms of his appointment.

This account of the six daughters of John Grey aims at describing them individually against the background of family life of the period. It is divided into nine chapters, which between them deal with three principal topics, namely:

Parentage of the nine Grey children,
Upbringing and Environment of the six sisters,
Their Menfolk and Progeny.

The term "Victorian" was adopted in the 1850s to describe a new self-consciousness. It appeared in *The Age and Its Architects*, by E.P. Hood, published in 1851. All six girls were born before the Coronation of Queen

Victoria on 28 June 1838 and they went into the world on marriage early in her long reign. The eldest of the six was born in 1819 and married in 1836. The youngest was born in 1836 and married in 1856. They can therefore aptly be described as Early Victorians.

There is a considerable two-volume work entitled *Early Victorian England 1830-65;* edited by G.M. Young and published by the Oxford University Press in 1934, with a third impression in 1963. This work covers a period which corresponds approximately with the second period of thirty years in the working life of John Grey, from 1833-63, which was noted above.

At the conclusion of *Early Victorian England* the years 1830-65 are described as follows:

"The period might be defined variously. It was the age of the ten pound householder whose importance was determined by the Reform Act of 1832. Industrially, it opened with the invention of railway transport. It saw the invention of the electric telegraph and great strides in English agriculture. The contributors to the work aimed at providing the background of the ideas and habits of early Victorian England. In their judgement the Early Victorian Age would be recognised in History."

This is thought to be an apt description

of the period and it fits in with the author's conception of it.

*Early Victorian England* refers specifically to Elizabeth Fry (1780–1845) and Florence Nightingale (1820–1910). It is surprising to find that there is no reference to Josephine Butler (1828–1906), a contemporary Early Victorian and, in the opinion of many, no less eminent. A possible explanation of this omission is tendered in the Epilogue.

This account contains references to some places in Northumberland which are in themselves unimportant. As they may be difficult to find on a map, the reader is referred to the locality, which was known at the time as a Ward. In the reign of Queen Victoria, in England, as a whole, a County was not primarily an administrative area, its main concern being justice and highways. In the 1830s, Northumberland contained six administrative regions called Wards, which were named after geographical features. In the north-west of the County, the Border area constituted Glendale Ward which took its name from the River Glen. The north-east Ward was named Bambrough (sic) after the town. In the middle of Northumberland on the west side was Coquetdale Ward, which took its name from the River Coquet. To the east of it was Morpeth Ward, which took its name from the town of Morpeth. Tindale Ward, in the south-west derived its name from the two tributaries of the Tyne, the North Tyne and South Tyne. To the east of it was Castle Ward which incorporated Newcastle-on-Tyne.

The above information is derived from a map of Northumberland dated 1831 in the Pocket County Maps Series published by Chapman & Hall, 186 Strand. This map also shows the Mail and Coach Roads.

## CHAPTER II

## PARENTAGE OF THE GREY CHILDREN

The six Grey sisters and their three brothers were the offspring of John Grey and his wife Hannah Eliza, daughter of Ralph Annett of Alnwick. John Grey belonged to a Northumbrian family which had long been associated with the Border Country. The parents of John Grey were George Grey (1754-1791) and Mary Burn (1759-1827), daughter of John Burn of Berwick-on-Tweed, who were married in 1782.

John Grey's branch of the family had farmed land at Long Horsley, six miles north of Morpeth. In 1788 George Grey had bought land at West Ord on the banks of the Tweed. Later he bought and cleared land at Milfield in Glendale Ward. George Grey died in 1791 at the early age of thirty-eight, leaving Mary a widow, with two sons and two daughters to bring up. John, born on 23 August 1785, was the eldest; next was Margaretta born 6 January 1787; then Mary born 6 November 1788, and lastly, George born 26 June 1790.

Mary Grey was a woman of energy and ability. She managed the estate and brought up her young children, looking after their early education herself. She was well-read and took steps to see that her children received a good education. This is how Josephine Butler described her grandmother in her book *Memoir* of

*John Grey of Dilston:*

"She was a woman worthy to be remembered. She was very thoughtful and studious. She read a great deal with her children, and also alone. Her practical energy, which was great, was called out in the care, now devolving entirely on her, of her farm, work-people and stock. She attended to everything herself, and while engaged in active household work, she would challenge her children to trials of memory by recitations from Pope's Homer. Her acquaintance with literature made her an authority with the promoters of the Wooler Library, to whom she supplied lists of books. She was slender and graceful in figure, quick and active in all her movements, an excellent rider and much admired on horseback. She had rich chestnut hair and a kind face, full of bright intelligence."

John Grey's School-days.

For some years John and his brother and sisters had a tutor, after which John was sent to Richmond School where he spent two or three years, from 1799-1801.

This period was of great importance in the life of John Grey largely on account of the personality of the Master of the School, James Tate. He was born in Richmond and was educated at

Richmond School and Sidney Sussex College, Cambridge, of which he ultimately became a Fellow. He returned to Richmond School as Master in 1796 and remained there until 1833, acquiring a reputation as a Classical Scholar and inspiring teacher. His impact on the school was soon felt. About 1805 two sons of Earl Grey attended the school. Not only did John Grey receive a classical education but he had the opportunity of learning about agriculture. As he boarded with the Master during the holidays, as well as in term-time, he made the acquaintance of men with practical experience of agriculture and a reputation as successful farmers belonging to three families: Collings, Charges and Booths.

After leaving Richmond School John Grey went to study under a Mr. Sewell, described as a good, but not active or enlightened clergyman, who lived at Lorton in Cumberland. In letters to his mother John recounted following the Lorton Hounds on foot, feasts and country gatherings, interspersing his descriptions with quotations from English and Latin poems. Emily, his youngest daughter, recalled how her father took her to see Lorton, the quiet village where he had stayed as a boy, and showed her the ancient yew tree in which he used to sit and study Virgil and Homer.

In 1803, after two years at Lorton, John Grey returned to Milfield, and, although only eighteen years of age, took over the management of the family estates. In the same year Mary Grey arranged, with her son's agreement, to send her daughters, Margaretta and Mary, to a school near London called Flint House. Margaretta was then sixteen and Mary fifteen. Both remained at school for several years.

## The Family Home at Milfield Hill.

Some time after her husband's death in 1791 Mary Grey moved with her children to a house on the hill at Milfield village, hence the name Milfield Hill. It stood at the end of the village and had large stone pillars at the corners of the garden wall. It was on the coach road from London to Edinburgh along which the mail coach passed daily; it was named Queen Charlotte, after the wife of King George III. In later years the children of John Grey and his wife used to go along a lane to the point where the mail bags were thrown off, in order to obtain the latest news brought by the London Express Coach.

On 12 October 1808, soon after returning home from school, Margaretta Grey married her cousin, Henry Grey D.D., a minister of the Church of Scotland who later entered the Free Church on its secession in 1843. Margaretta was to exercise considerable influence on her brother and also her niece Josephine.

John Grey, when he took charge of the Milfield Hill estate in 1803, was determined to make a success of farming.

He studied agriculture in theory and practice, taking advice from neighbouring farmers, in particular a well-known landowner and close friend, George Culley. From his early years John Grey experimented in schemes aiming at improving soil through drainage and the use of fertilisers, and at the betterment of livestock. In the spring of 1814 he travelled in Holland, Belgium, Germany and France to gain experience of their methods of agriculture. He was then aged twenty-nine.

The Marriage of John Grey.

On 27 December 1814 John Grey married Hannah Eliza, daughter of Ralph Annett of The Fence, near Alnwick. He first met her in a chance equestrian encounter the previous winter. In the course of a long ride on horseback in wintry conditions he had alighted at a country inn. She had dismounted from her horse to rest. Other encounters on horseback led to a romance and to their wedding at Alnwick. The bride came riding to church, dressed in a pale-blue riding habit richly embroidered. Both her parents were devout Protestants of Huguenot stock.

In the course of eighteen years at Milfield Hill, from 1815-1833, John Grey and his wife reared a family of eight children, three boys and five girls. A sixth daughter was born to them after they had moved from Milfield Hill to Dilston near the River Tyne, in 1835.

At an early stage in his farming career John Grey entered into correspondence with leading agriculturists and especially Sir John Sinclair (1754–1835) who was the first President of the Board of Agriculture and author of a highly-publicised *Code of Agriculture*, and Arthur Young (1741–1820), the Secretary of the Board since 1793. The latter was pre-eminent among writers on agriculture. He published forty-five Annals of Agriculture from 1784 and toured England, Wales and France. He died at the age of eighty and was totally blind for the last ten years but his influence on agriculture was undiminished.

John Grey was also associated with other agriculturists in setting up Agricultural Societies, prominent among them being the Union Agricultural Society formed by the amalgamation of the Tweedside Society with the Border Society of Kelso.

Political Activities of John Grey.

Farming activities did not preoccupy John Grey to the exclusion of other things when living at Milfield Hill. At an early stage of his life there as landowner and tenant farmer he took an active part in local politics. He was an ardent supporter of the Whig Party which, under the leadership of certain well-known landowners, notably Lord Grey and Lord Durham, was challenging the dominant Tory party in Northumberland. In his own locality John Grey campaigned

11

actively in support of certain major issues, especially the abolition of slavery, electoral reform, the Poor Law, free trade in corn. The slave trade had been prohibited in 1807 but slave-holding as it existed in the West Indies was debated from 1823 to 1833, when it was prohibited. During this period John Grey was a leading member of the local Anti-Slavery Committee. He took a prominent part in the campaign to do away with rotten boroughs and enfranchise ten pound householders. The Reform Bill of June 1832 was passed only as a result of the dissolution of the House of Lords by King William IV in the near-revolutionary situation preceding the fall of the Tory Government. In this critical period Earl Grey, the Whig Prime Minister, used to sound John Grey about public opinion in Northumberland.

John Grey appointed Receiver.

The year 1833 was a turning point in John Grey's life. In 1831 a Whig Government had come to power. It continued in office for three years under Earl Grey, with short periods under Lord Melbourne. In 1832 an important agricultural post had become vacant in Northumberland. The post was that of administrator of estates which had been forfeited by the Radcliffe family in the eighteenth century. The story of the Radcliffe family's downfall is a sad episode in Northumberland's history.

In the sixteenth century the Radcliffe

family converted an old castle at Dilston, on a small tributary of the River Tyne named Devil's Water, into an Elizabethan manor. In 1622 Sir Francis Radcliffe added to it a mansion called Dilston Hall and a chapel. The Earl of Derwentwater took up residence in 1714. In 1715 he took part in the Rising in support of the Old Pretender. He was taken prisoner and was executed. His brother, Charles Radcliffe, escaped from prison and fled abroad. Later he returned to England clandestinely and took part in the abortive 1745 Rebellion. In October 1745 a small force marched on Newcastle but after reaching Hexham it withdrew to Scotland. Charles Radcliffe was captured in a minor engagement and was later executed. The Radcliffe estates, which had been sequestrated in 1716, were held by Trustees until 1735 when they were handed over to Greenwich Hospital. In 1832 the administration of the estates was judged to be unsatisfactory and Earl Grey offered John Grey the post of Commissioner, or Receiver, for all the Hospital's estates in Northumberland and Cumberland. John Grey accepted the appointment and assumed responsibility for the estates in 1833. The bulk of the property was on Tyneside and centred on Corbridge and Dilston, but John Grey did not move his family south until two years later as accommodation on the property was lacking.

# CHAPTER III

## UPBRINGING OF THE FAMILY

The upbringing of John Grey's children can be reconstructed from two principal sources; Emily Grey's *Recollections*, written early in the present century, which were briefly referred to by A.S.G. Butler in his *Portrait of Josephine Butler* (p.55); and Josephine Butler's book about her father, *Memoir of John Grey of Dilston*. There is sufficient information about the second period from 1833 onwards but information about the early years at Milfield Hill is sparse.

Upbringing at Milfield Hill.

There was an age-gap of twenty-one years between the eldest daughter, known as Eliza although christened Hannah Eliza, and Emily. The four older Grey children spent their most impressionable years at Milfield Hill. They were: George, John, Eliza and Mary Ann. They were brought up on what was a large farm, with its advantages and dis-advantages. They received only a fair education. They learnt to ride young and cultivated a love of animals. George, the eldest son, took over the Milfield Hill estate from his father in 1833 and never lived at Dilston. When the move to Dilston took place in 1835 John was eighteen, Eliza sixteen and Mary Ann fourteen. Fanny was twelve, Josephine seven and Harriet five. Eliza was

married on 13 September 1836, within a
year of the move to Dilston. Emily had
been born three months earlier, on 27
May, at Dilston. It is believed that the
boys had a tutor at Milfield Hill and
they may have attended school but the
foundation of the girls' education was
laid by their mother, Hannah Grey,
herself. Harriet, the fifth daughter, in
later life paid a tribute to her mother:
"What a beautiful handwriting our Mother
had and such a wise and dignified
manner of expressing herself". Although
the four older girls lacked certain
advantages at Milfield Hill, they looked
back nostalgically on their days there.

The Move to Dilston.
    The administration of the Greenwich
Hospital Estates was conducted from
Dilston near Corbridge. At the time of
his appointment to the post of Receiver
John Grey was living at Milfield Hill,
which was fifty miles away from Dilston,
and he was compelled to occupy
temporary lodgings on Tyneside, leaving
the family behind. It was decided,
however, to build a house on the estate
as a residence and office for the use of
the Receiver, and John Grey and his wife
were invited to choose the site. They
chose the site on which Dilston Hall
stands today, about fifty yards from the
ruins of the Castle on the right bank of
Devil's Water. This mountain stream is a
tributary of the Tyne and the house is
about two miles upstream from its

confluence with the Tyne. A.S.G. Butler, in his book about Josephine Butler, was mistaken in saying that the house was on the Tyne; he wrote (p.34) "the family lived at Dilston overlooking the Tyne near Corbridge. A new house was built there".

## Upbringing at Dilston Hall.

The house built for the Receiver of the Greenwich Hospital Estates and his family was commodious and comfortable and stood in beautiful surroundings. It was designed to house a family employing a considerable domestic staff and to include office accommodation, described as "business rooms", for the Receiver and his assistants. Dilston Hall was visited by the author and his wife in September 1980 and it looks today just as it was portrayed in a sepia drawing by the talented Fanny Grey in her album of sketches dated 1848. Today Dilston Hall is occupied by an Advanced Social Training Unit of the National Society for Mentally Handicapped Children, whose Director is G. Franklin Gray. When John Grey and his family moved into their new home in 1835 it was known as Dilston House.

## A Boarding-school Education for the Girls.

It is noteworthy that there was a predilection in the Grey family for a boarding-school education. This was at a time when it was rare for daughters to be sent away from home to be educated.

Mary Grey, John Grey's mother, sent her two daughters to a boarding-school near London because she herself was taken up with the affairs of the estate. Margaretta, the elder, was an enthusiastic supporter of education for women as was John Grey, her brother. They both rejected the tendency, current in the eighteenth century, to assume that young ladies should be brought up at home to look decorative and acquire certain social accomplishments, as they thought that this could only lead to them leading useless lives and they considered that a good education for young women was indispensable. Josephine Butler was greatly influenced by her aunt Margaretta and became a fervent supporter of education for women, including a university education.

After the family's move to Dilston, Hannah Grey was too preoccupied with domestic affairs to play a large part in her children's education. Emily was taught by a nursery governess to start with and all the girls went to a boarding-school in succession. This is not to say that Hannah Grey did not play a part in her children's upbringing. Josephine Butler paid this eloquent tribute to her mother:

"We owed so much to our dear Mother, who was very firm in requiring from us that whatever we did should be thoroughly done, and that in taking up any study we should aim at becoming as perfect as we could, without external aid. This was a moral discipline which perhaps compensated in value for the lack of a great store of knowledge. She would assemble us daily for the reading aloud of some solid book and, by a kind of examination following the reading, assure herself that we had mastered the subject. She urged us to aim at excellence, if not perfection, in at least one thing."

At School in Newcastle.

After the family had settled at Dilston House a school was found at Newcastle-on-Tyne to which to send each of the girls on reaching a certain age. Emily Grey in her *Recollections* recalled her school-days. She said that she had been preceded by her four sisters – Mary Ann, Fanny, Josephine and Hatty. Josephine Butler wrote in her book *In Memoriam – Harriet Meuricoffre*, "For two years my sister (Hatty) and I were together at a school in Newcastle." This was misconstrued by Miss E. Moberly Bell, as it had also been by A.S.G. Butler, into assuming that two years education was all that the school could provide. The fact is that Fanny and Josephine were star pupils at the school and were there for several years. Josephine, being two years older than Hatty, had preceded her at school and Hatty, who did not like school, left after only two years.

Emily went to the school when aged

ten and enjoyed her school-days which lasted over several years. The school was run by a Miss Tidy and the girls were looked after by a kind old housekeeper. Both of them were very kind to Emily, although her work was patchy. She indulged her passion for history and music, learning to play the piano, but mathematics were beyond her. Life at the school sounds as if it had been a very normal one. Tuck boxes were kept in the attic and food received from home was shared with friends. The newly installed train service made visiting easier on the part of the girls' mother and their brother Charles, who was at Durham University.

## The Ménage at Dilston.

The domestic staff at Dilston Hall, as it came to be known, were all females as John Grey thought that male servants were prone to demand to be waited on by female staff. The staff comprised a cook, nurse, nursery governess and several maids. Outside staff, who also had to be accommodated, included a coachman, groom and stable lads. They were all needed because only horse transport was available to enable John Grey to make his tours of inspection in Northumberland and because the whole family were horse and animal lovers. There was at least one gardener but there were no elaborate gardens to be maintained.

Dependence on Horses.

Northumberland was shortly to see the introduction of a railway system, and in this respect Northumberland and Durham were ahead of the greater part of England, although well behind Scotland. Nevertheless, public transport was still horse-drawn in the early 1830s and a map of 1831 shows that there were few arterial roads in Northumberland. There was a Mail Road up the east coast and one across the County from Newcastle to Carlisle. There was an Express Coach Road from Newcastle via Rothbury, in Coquetdale Ward, to Kelso in Scotland and beyond. There were in addition a number of coach roads. Conveyances of different kinds were required by the Grey family for journeys that could not be covered on horseback, the mode of travel most favoured by John Grey himself. At Dilston Hall there was a gig, a light two-wheeled vehicle; a two-wheeled dog-cart with cross seats back to back for four persons; a phaeton or light four-wheeled carriage drawn by a pair of horses, and a four-wheeled carriage with ample luggage room also drawn by two horses. The frequent journey of fifty miles from Dilston to Milfield Hill was normally made in an open gig with one night stop.

Staff Relations.

The happy relationship existing between family and staff at Dilston Hall led to some of the staff remaining in service for very long periods. Jane Batson, Emily's nursery governess, was a helper and friend of the family until her death at an advanced old age. There was a devoted old groom, James by name. The Greys' faithful coachman, Cranston, had married a certain Jane who had been nurse to the older children since the childhood of Frances Hardy (Fanny) at Milfield Hill. After Cranston retired, he and his wife kept an Inn at Alston, in Tindale Ward, where John Grey used to stay the night when visiting the lead mines in the company of one of his daughters. Jane Cranston died very soon after her mistress, Hannah Grey. Josephine Butler wrote of her:

"Dear faithful Jane! This faithful nurse well deserved to be named in a family history. My father or mother would often visit her alone in the nursery at night after all the children were asleep in order to confer with her on matters of difficulty or of the deepest concern to the family."

Religious Influences.

Both John Grey and his wife were brought up in the Christian faith. Hannah Grey belonged to a family which was deeply religious. This is how Josephine Butler wrote about her grandmother in a letter to her grandson when he was at Rugby; the year was not given but it was probably 1905. Here is a quotation:

"My mother's parents were descendants of the persecuted Huguenots, silk weavers, so many of whom were driven out of France in the reign of Louis XIV. They were such good people. Their name was Annett. They were poor but so good. They lived at a house called The Fence near Alnwick. They used to receive in their humble home missionaries or evangelists of all kinds. They sent my mother to a Moravian school in Yorkshire. The Moravians were among the earliest and bravest of Christian missionaries and they had such a joyous faith. Everything was done with music. Funerals were all singing processions dressed in white. They never had black dresses. It was there that my mother learned to be such a first-rate classical musician. She was the pupil of Christian Ignatius Latrobe, a composer of sacred music. She played so well, both piano and harp, and it was she who always urged me on to practise and made of me something of a musician."

Hannah Grey's parents were not members of the Moravian Church and their choice of school for their daughter was dictated by the fact that they wanted her to

22

receive a boarding-school education with a religious background. They sent her to a Moravian boarding-school at Fulneck, near Leeds. The Moravians are a Protestant episcopal Church, a continuation of the Bohemian Brethren who were expelled from Bohemia in the seventeenth century. They spread into Germany, England and North America, engaging in missionary work. Christian Latrobe, who was born in Fulneck in 1757 was the son of Benjamin Latrobe, a Superintendent of the Moravian Brethren in England. He himself was a Minister in the Moravian Church. He composed and edited much church music for the Moravians and also some for Anglican congregations. He was probably music master at the local school.

The school which Hannah attended is still at Fulneck. Founded in 1753, it is now named Fulneck Girls School, its address being Pudsey, West Yorkshire. This Boarding and Day School is under the Directing Body of the Moravian Church and aims at providing a liberal education based on Christian principles. Fulneck Boys School at Pudsey is conducted on similar lines.

The Visions of Margaret Annett

Josephine Butler wrote a letter to her grandson about Hannah Grey's mother, Margaret, wife of Ralph Annett of Alnwick. Josephine wrote as follows:

"Some names which I had forgotten in telling you of my maternal

grandmother's 'visions', came back
to my memory when you had gone.
The ship which was burnt in mid-
ocean was the Kent East Indiaman
of sad renown. Some few of the
sailors must have escaped to tell
the tale, and were perhaps picked
up by another boat, but the Kent
East Indiaman perished completely..
...some of my grandmother's visions
were very wonderful and all came
true."

A list of notable shipwrecks states "The
Kent, an East Indiaman, burnt in the
Bay of Biscay in 1825. Nearly all were
saved by the brig Cambria". Mrs. Annett
would have been in her middle fifties at
the time of this occurrence.

John Grey's Example.
  The Grey household was a soberly
Christian one. Family prayers, which
were attended by the domestic staff, were
held daily. John Grey was a regular
attender at the Parish Church of St.
Andrew's, Corbridge. Josephine described
the family routine as follows:

"Two miles from our home was the
Parish Church, to which we trudged
dutifully every Sunday and where
an honest man in the pulpit taught
us loyally all that he probably
himself knew about God."

The religious background of the girls'

life at Dilston Hall did not result in their being put off from religion. Their subsequent lives indicated that the reverse was the case. They acquired from their father an interest in people and social questions. They had affection and respect for him, recognising his sense of justice, robustness, warm-heartedness and generosity.

John Grey was a man of simple habits, abstemious where drinking of wine was concerned and with a strong prejudice against smoking. In 1830, and for many years after, a man was by convention debarred from smoking in the presence of ladies. The usual smoke of the time was a pipe and, for the minority who could afford it, a cigar. Cigars were introduced into England by soldiers returning from the Spanish Peninsular Wars, during which they ha picked up the habit from French soldiers, who, in their turn, had acquired it from the Spanish. A cigarette, or "paper cigar smoking," as it was first known, was not practised in England until after the Crimean War. In 1840 smoking in railway carriages or on stations was forbidden. Until the 1850s smoking was rarely allowed in a respectable house. The idea of a smoking-room was developed in the late 1840s. Osborne House in the Isle of Wight, built in 1845 for Queen Victoria, contained a "smoking room" to meet the requirements of Prince Albert.

Pastimes and Accomplishments of the Sisters.

The girls' upbringing was far from being staid and conventional. They were fond of dancing and parties. The County Ball at Alnwick was a great occasion. They loved horses and availed themselves of opportunities for hunting, as when they visited their brother, George Grey, at Milfield Hill. He was Master of Hounds, a magistrate and a Deputy Lieutenant for the County of Northumberland.

The environment at Dilston enabled the girls freely to pursue their individual interests. A lead in flower tending was given by Hannah Grey who had a small walled garden of her own. She encouraged Emily to emulate her. Young ladies of this period set great store by flowers. To press flowers and arrange them in an album, or to paint them with their Latin names inscribed beneath, were fashionable pursuits at the time. Carolus Linnaeus (1707–1778), a Swedish botanist, had devised a concise method of naming plants and animals by *genus* and species. He used Latin for his system of classification which he set out in *Species Plantarum* in 1753. A Linnean Society based on collections of Linnaeus, was founded in 1788 by Sir J.E. Smith. This collection is now housed in the Linnean Rooms in Burlington House.

There is with the author a small album of pressed flowers which dates from about 1840 and was almost certainly the work of Frances Hardy (Fanny), possibly with other sisters co-operating. The flowers have lost none of their colour and represent a quite remarkable technique.

Fanny Grey was artistic and Josephine reckoned that, with training, she could have developed into a real artist. Her album, dated 1848, contains sepia drawings of great charm of Dilston and the Northumbrian countryside; also some paintings of flowers, with their Latin names inscribed.

Josephine had considerable skill as a painter but did not develop it, possibly because her husband, George Butler, was himself a talented artist. He gave her a very fine paintbox in about 1864. This is how A.S.G. Butler described it in his book about his grandmother:

"A large walnut box, beautifully made, lined with red leather. There are neatly fitting compartments for all the appliances, but the real thrill is the secret drawer in the false bottom containing a variety of china palettes and finest sable brushes. It is the sort of box which would have been carried about by a manservant. Obviously it has been little used; and that fits with what I recall of my grandmother's actual drawing. She was very swift, rarely rubbed out and was indifferent to the qualities of pencils or paper. Hence those

brushes are in her box today and I
use them perpetually."

Andrew Butler was himself an artist of
some repute. He used the brushes and
there is nothing left of them, but the
box, initialled J.E.B. on the lid, retains
its elegance.

# CHAPTER IV

## THEN EXISTING PUBLIC SERVICES

Introduction of Steam Trains.

The Grey sisters were born into a period of rapid change as a result of inventions which affected their whole way of life. Northumberland and Durham were the first counties to benefit from the introduction of steam trains. Interest in steam was first manifested in a Northumberland colliery where George Stephenson (1781-1848) was an engine-wright. He built his first engine in 1814 and this led to him being appointed engineer to the Stockton-Darlington Railway. This railway began by carrying goods only. The first passenger-carrying railway was the Liverpool-Manchester line which began to function in 1830.

Cheap transport was needed to convey coal, iron and lead from source to river. The easiest route across England in the North was the line of the Mail Road from Carlisle to Newcastle, which passed through Hexham and Corbridge. The first railway across England was the Newcastle-Carlisle Railway which received its Act in 1839. Its trace passed through Hexham and Corbridge, crossing the River Tyne at Corbridge to avoid the danger of flooding. When the line was open in 1839 it passed within a few hundred yards of Dilston Hall, for which a private station was built. Emily Grey recalls in her *Recollections* that visitors to Dilston Hall used this station and that their luggage was transported in a small cart pulled by a pony which was left in England by Eliza Morrison when she and her family left for Hong Kong in 1847. The luggage was handled by the station–master, a railway pensioner with a wooden leg, called Old Joe, who would comment caustically on any suitor of one of his "young ladies" of whom he did not approve.

Until the middle of the nineteenth century the journey from Edinburgh to London via Newcastle had to be made by coach where Northumberland was concerned. In 1828 this journey cost fifty pounds, a very big sum in those days. In 1850 the link between Edinburgh and London was completed on the opening of the Royal Border Bridge at Berwick-on-Tweed which was designed by Robert Stephenson (1803–1859), son of George Stephenson. John Grey was personally acquainted with George Stephenson, and Josephine Butler, in her book, quoted her father's description of him: "Our north–country genius, George Stephenson, whose snow–white hair, fine dark eyes, black eyebrows and open brow made him easily recognisable in a crowd". The introduction of railways led to more and cheaper travel. In 1844 Parliament obliged railway companies to run cheap trains daily. Excursions were introduced in 1845 by Thomas Cook.

## Postal Facilities.

Postal facilities were also much improved in the first half of the nineteenth century. Before 1784 mail outside London was carried by post-boys on horseback. Then mail coaches were introduced, the mail being handed over by post-masters to armed guards, for fear of highwaymen. In 1824 a letter by mail coach travelled four hundred miles in a period of forty hours at a cost of one shilling, which was a considerable sum. Before Penny Post was introduced in 1840, postage was paid by the recipient at a rate which varied according to distance. In London there was a two-penny post. In the middle of the century long-distance mail was entrusted to railways.

Newspapers were carried as mail. There was a stamp-duty on them which in 1836, was lowered by the Whig Administration from four pence to one penny.

## The Press.

In her *Recollections* Emily described how her father, at the end of a busy day sometimes involving hours of riding, used to sit reading the daily paper and impart scraps of information to her. The position of the press in the first half of the nineteenth century is sometimes underestimated. It played an important part in the political debates of the period. The Times was in circulation as early as 1815. The Sunday papers anticipated daily papers, and, in the early part of the nineteenth century, had greater influence. There were a number of distinguished political writers, especially William Hazlitt; Barnes, the independent editor of The Times; and William Cobbett (1762-1835) who conducted a Weekly Political Register for thirty-three years. He was an ardent supporter of the unfortunate Queen Caroline, wife of King George IV, and a warm advocate of Parliamentary Reform. Coleridge was a regular contributor to the Morning Post. The circulation of the Sunday papers had reached one hundred thousand by 1829 but the combined sales of the daily papers published in London were considerably less. Daily newspapers cost seven pence a day, the modern equivalent of something under one pound, and were therefore out of reach of the bulk of society. A limiting factor was a stamp-duty. It was lowered by the Whig Administration in 1836 from four pence to one penny and was repealed in 1855. This led to a large increase in circulation. The Daily Telegraph began as a two-penny paper that year but soon became London's first penny paper.

The Electric Telegraph.

An invention of outstanding importance was the electric telegraph. It was employed from 1838 onwards but it only became available to the general public in the 1850s.

The Lack of Communications.

Some episodes in the life of the Grey family show how very much everyday life was affected by lack of communications. John Grey's younger brother, George (1790-1824) had in 1813 married in Edinburgh, Jane, daughter of John Gregson of Belchester and moved to Surrey to farm there. He was attractive and popular but somewhat careless and wayward. In October 1824 he was thrown from his horse or carriage and grievously injured. The news was sent to Milfield Hill but John Grey was away on business in Edinburgh. He was returning by coach when the guard of the north-bound coach, which crossed it, whispered to his colleague that George Grey was dead. This was John Grey's first inkling of the fatal accident.

John Grey's second son, John Henry, was an invalid, having had an accident which caused a rib to penetrate the lung. In 1844 he set sail in a ship bound for Hong Kong, for a change of air and to stay with his sister, Eliza Morrison, but he died on the way out. On arrival in China, the captain of the ship reported the fact, saying: "All well, except Mr. Grey, who died off the Cape". It was only after some months that a letter, written by a young sailor who had acted as servant to John Henry, brought details of his death to his family.

# CHAPTER V

## REMINISCENCES OF CHILDHOOD by
## Mrs. THOMAS

John Grey was fortunate in that he was endowed with strength and good health and had an exceptionally good memory, described by one of his daughters as "prodigious". It was not dimmed even in old age as is shown by his correspondence with his children and grandchildren. The gift of a good memory was inherited by Josephine and Emily, as is clear from their writings.

The Recollections of Emily Thomas (née Grey).

Emily's *Recollections*, written when she was at an advanced age, vividly describe certain episodes in her young life. She claimed to have been difficult as a child and her reminiscences reveal that she was impetuous, unconventional and restless in her youth.

Love of Animals.

Emily, being much the youngest, was left to her own devices. She developed a love of animals and especially of horses and dogs. This formed a special link with her father. He was not only a good horseman but a good judge of horses. Emily recalled how John Grey had seen in Newcastle a drove of Highland ponies going to work in the pits. He noticed a beautiful snow-white pony and was

34

unhappy to think it would be condemned to a life of labour and darkness in a coal-mine. He negotiated its purchase with the driver and it was brought to Dilston Hall where it soon became a family pet. It was ridden by the two youngest girls but was also used to draw a low phaeton. It lived to be twenty-eight.

Emily recalled that Colonel Charles Grey, who was Private Secretary to Prince Albert, wrote to John Grey asking him to select and buy a horse for Princess Alice, one which was well-trained for the moors and timber in Scotland. Emily and her father kept a look-out and eventually found a creamy-grey animal which was out to grass and untrained, the property of a paper manufacturer at Shotley. It was bought and taken to Dilston. This young horse, which was spirited but sweet-tempered, was ridden daily by Emily. To make it sure-footed, she schooled it in a thick wood of six hundred acres and in rocky places. Creamlaid, as the horse was called, was sent to Princess Alice at Balmoral. Colonel Grey wrote to say that she was delighted with Creamlaid, which eventually became her favourite horse for that country. This was probably in 1851 or 1852 when Princess Alice was eight or nine years old.

A Dog called Darling.

Adjoining the stables at Dilston Hall was a yard called Darling's Yard because it housed a red retriever of that name, which was Emily's constant companion. John Grey had paid a visit to the Farne Islands off Berwick, numbering twenty-five, associated with the name of Grace Darling. She was the daughter of a lighthouse keeper there. On 7 September 1838 the *Forfarshire*, en route from Hull to Dundee, was wrecked a mile away. Grace Darling rowed with her father in a small boat to the wreck through a raging sea, taking their dog with them. They saved nine lives and Grace Darling was awarded a medal for her courage. She was born at Bamburgh and that is where her tomb is. The son of the lighthouse keeper's dog was given to John Grey in appreciation of his visit to the Islands and it was consequently, if somewhat inappropriately, named Darling.

Queen Victoria's Rail Journey from Balmoral.

In a letter to her eldest sister Eliza, in Hong Kong, Emily described how the Royal Family had entrained at Little Mills station near Alnwick in Morpeth Ward on their way from Balmoral to London. Emily had been staying with her sister, Fanny Smyttan, and was driven by a fellow guest, the Curate at Hawick, in his phaeton to the newly-opened railway station. The Royal Family had been staying the night with Lord and Lady Grey at Hawick Hall, and were driven in an open carriage to Little Mills where a large crowd from Alnwick had assembled to see the Queen. The year was probably 1850. Queen Victoria and Prince Albert had become enamoured of Balmoral on their first visit in 1848 and had arranged to lease an old castle, which was extensively modified according to plans of Prince Albert in the course of the next few years. They went with their children to Balmoral in 1849 and 1850, travelling by sea on both occasions, as they had done in 1848. The North of England was in an unsettled state and a sea-journey was deemed to be less hazardous even though it may have been more uncomfortable. Queen Victoria's descriptions of the journeys in her personal journal reveal that the whole family succumbed to sea-sickness.

The Queen must have been travelling south after staying at Balmoral. The Royal Family had attended the Braemar Gathering on 12 September 1850 and they would have been able to travel all the way back to Windsor by train as the rail link from Edinburgh to Newcastle and beyond was completed as a result of the opening of the Royal Bridge at Berwick-on-Tweed on 28 August 1850.

A Visit to France.

In 1853, Emily, then seventeen years old, was taken by her brother George and his wife on a visit to France. In 1851 Napoleon Bonaparte had been re-elected President as a result of a military coup and in 1852 he was proclaimed Emperor Napoleon the Third.

During their stay in Paris the Grey party happened to be at Versailles when the Emperor held a review of troops. He rode up the broadwalk of the magnificent gardens, flanked by his bodyguard of gentlemen in colourful uniforms. Emily had the temerity to step forward and touch his stirrup as he passed, saying "Long live the Emperor". Napoleon smiled and slightly raised his General's hat. On a later occasion Emily saw Empress Eugenie being driven in an open carriage, accompanied by Prince Jerome Bonaparte, President of the Senate. The Empress was then at the height of her popularity. Emily rated her the most beautiful woman she had ever seen.

The Great Exhibition, 1851.

An event of great importance in stimulating rail travel was the Great Exhibition in London, known as Prince Albert's Exhibition, which opened on 1 May 1851. The plan was first considered by the Royal Society of Arts, which met under Prince Albert's Presidency in July 1849, and in 1850 a Royal Commission was appointed to organise the Exhibition. Cheap rail travel to London was introduced. John Grey availed himself of it to arrange for his wife, their son Charles, Hatty and Emily to go up to London for the Exhibition and to go to places of entertainment. They stayed in rooms in Manchester Square.

Emily was then just fifteen and she wrote ecstatically about the Exhibition which evoked great enthusiasm. It was visited by over six million persons, a daily average of over forty-three thousand. Emily was able to enlarge her interest in music and the musical world. In 1846 her mother had taken her to see a performance in Newcastle of Bellini's opera, Norma, in which Grisi, the well-known singer, and Mario, her husband, had performed. In London Emily heard Luigi Lablache (1794-1858) in the Barber of Seville and Henry IV and she also saw Madame Vestris (1797-1856) act in King Charming. Madame Vestris and her husband, Charles Mathews, dominated the theatre in London from 1831-1854. Vestris was already fifty but still looked enchanting as she used to go to Paris twice a year to be enamelled. Emily was struck by Grisi's loveliness and recorded with appreciation the reputation which she and her husband had earned for leading a tranquil home life with their children and for their open-handedness at Musgrave House in Fulham.

A Prize Grand Piano.

In the early part of the last century, skill on the piano was a principal accomplishment of young ladies. Devotion to Handel was followed by devotion to Mendelssohn and later Beethoven. Mendelssohn paid his first visit to England in 1829 and performed on numerous occasions. He was especially popular with the Royal Family. Beethoven was studied from 1834 by advanced pupils. He wrote the Ninth Symphony for the Philharmonic Society.

The height of ambition of music-lovers was to have a pianoforte, or grand piano, and to be instructed by Sterndale Bennett, Professor of Music at Cambridge, whose pupils included Queen Victoria.

At the Great Exhibition there was a display of pianofortes. The display was staged by the firm of Erard, which was named after Sebastien Erard (1752–1831) who set up as a manufacturer of pianos in Paris and invented the grand piano with double escapement in 1823. Other exhibitors at the Exhibition were Collard & Collard, and Broadwood. There was a competition for the best pianoforte and a Broadwood Grand won the First Prize. It was presented to Josephine Butler as a wedding present on her marriage to George Butler. There is some uncertainty as to the donor. A.S.G. Butler says it was given by a rich uncle who paid two hundred guineas for it, but does not enlarge on it. Miss E. Moberly Bell, in her book about Josephine Butler, says it was bought at the Exhibition by "her cousin" Charles Grey and given to her as a wedding present, adding that Josephine took the opportunity of having piano lessons from Sterndale Bennett. It is doubtful whether there was a cousin of the name of Grey with the means to make so munificent a gift.

# CHAPTER VI

## CLOSING YEARS AT DILSTON HALL

Dilston Hall was a meeting place for members of the Grey family and their connections and, for a quarter of a century, John Grey had the means to help those of his daughters who needed it. He gave a home to Fanny after she had parted from her husband and to Emily, after the early death in 1860 of her first husband. In 1857 the situation changed markedly as John Grey suffered great loss from a bank failure. The Newcastle Bank, in which he was a shareholder, closed its doors as a result of certain dishonourable dealings within the management. John Grey was compelled to dispose of his paternal estate at Ord on Tweedside. He was greatly distressed about the resulting loss to his daughters, for whose future he had been making provision, but derived some comfort from the philosophical way in which his wife, Hannah, accepted the blow.

The Death of Hannah Grey.

On 15 May 1860 Hannah Grey, who had been in poor health for some years, died peacefully, but with very little warning. The only one of the family present was Emily who had been widowed earlier in the year. John Grey was at Alston collecting rents. He was advised that his wife was sinking and, there being no early train, he drove home with all haste but arrived two hours after his wife had ceased to breathe. The loss of his partner of forty-five years was a cruel blow.

## The Death of John Grey.

In 1863 John Grey retired at the age of seventy-seven. He left Dilston for a house at Lipwood on the bank of the Tyne, west of Dilston. It became a meeting place for his scattered off-spring. He had enjoyed wonderful health throughout his life and he was on horseback only a few days before his death, on 22 January 1868, at the age of eighty-two. He was buried by the side of his wife in the churchyard of St. Andrew's Corbridge, where all his six daughters had been given away in marriage by him.

## His Endearing Characteristics.

Josephine Butler, in her Memoir about her father, published the year after his death, wrote feelingly and frankly about her much-loved parents:

"It was happy for my father that the partner of his life possessed this hopefulness of character. He himself, though full of hope, which is sooner or later granted to the pure in heart, of the prevalence of good over evil, was constitution-ally rather sad, retrospective, apt to dwell with a tender melancholy on joys past, and friends departed, rather than to look forward; and withal somewhat diffident of his power."

Elsewhere Jospehine Butler wrote about John Grey: "He was a man of a somewhat mournful cast of mind; he was a man of progress nevertheless, sustained by a constant hope." Recalling her father's striving towards the end of his life not to give trouble to anyone, she wrote: "Such little foibles, together with a certain helplessness about small things and a want of skilfulness with his hands, endeared him the more to us. The tying of a neck-tie was a mystery he never could accomplish, with all his intelligence."

Tributes before Retirement.

In his tenure of office as Receiver of Greenwich Hospital Estates, John Grey was highly successful and greatly esteemed. Josephine Butler recorded in her *Memoir of John Grey* (page 202) that in 1849 a great number of friends and neighbours met to present him with a testimonial, not, in the words of the chairman,

"on the occasion of the conclusion of any term of office nor of any particular event but because his neighbours in the north could not for so long have been witnesses of his exertions in promoting the moral and material change which had come about in Tyneside of late

43

years – a work of which they must all be conscious was mainly the creation of one master mind – and feel themselves justified in withholding some such declaration of opinion as was before them."

A footnote to the account of this meeting of friends who presented a testimonial to John Grey stated that the presentation took the form of "various articles of silver–plate and an excellent portrait of himself by Patten (sic)." Richard Wilford in his biography of John Grey in *Men of Mark Twixt Tyne and Tweed 1895* ended his account by saying: "A full–size portrait of himself, by Patten (sic), was presented to Mr. Grey at the time of his removal from Dilston. It was afterwards exhibited in London and then placed in the New Hall at Hexham".

A Missing Portrait.

Assuming that the two references are to one and the same portrait of John Grey by the artist G. Patten, A.R.A., there is a discrepancy here since Wilford says the portrait was presented to him on his retirement from the post of Receiver, whereas the footnote in the Memoir implies that the date was 1849. Fortunately the date is verifiable by reference to an engraving of the portrait contained in a book entitled: *Josephine Butler – Her work and Principles and Their Meaning for the Twentieth Century.*

44

by Millicent G. Fawcett and E.M. Turner, published by The Association for Moral & Social Hygiene, London 1927. The caption to the illustration is "John Grey of Milfield Hill and of Dilston, Northumberland. From a portrait by G. Patten, A.R.A. July 1852." This established that the portrait was painted eleven years before the retirement of John Grey. A large engraving of the portrait now in the author's possession, gives additional details in the caption, which reads: "Painted by G. Patten, A.R.A. Engraved by G.J. Payne. Published July 1 1852 by R. Turner, Grey St. Newcastle." The portrait depicts John Grey as a man with a strong attractive face typifying the characteristics which have been attributed to him by those who knew him intimately.

The author communicated with Newcastle Central Library in the hope of establishing the present whereabouts of the portrait. The City Librarian replied that the painting had indeed been presented to Newcastle Corporation in about 1850 but its present whereabouts are not known. A communication by the author to Hexham elicited the reply from Tynedale District Council, Hexham House, that the painting was not in the Council's possession and that nothing was known about it. Should the portrait still be in existence, this reference to it might, conceivably, lead to it being identified, brought out of obscurity and appropriately housed.

A Tribute after Retirement.

Many tributes were paid to John Grey on retirement from the post of Receiver. Among them was one by J. Chalmers Morton, a well-known writer on agriculture, author of *An Encyclopaedia of Agriculture*, and of *Farming Almanac*, He contributed an article on John Grey's achievements in the Oxford Journal of 1864. The following is an extract from this striking testimony by an expert:

"There is hardly any profession whose wise and successful prosecution tends more to the general welfare than that of the landowner. It depends a great deal on him whether his estate shall yield food, wages, and farm profit in abundance, or at all. On his will and judgment rests the share which is contributed by his portion of the island to the prosperity of its population. There cannot be greater contrasts than land managed under different ownerships presents, – much greater than those arising out of difference of soil or of climate. The character of the ownership acts directly on the character of the population, producing all the difference between listlessness and energy, between poverty and wealth. There are light sandy districts in this country, formerly so worthless and deserted that land lighthouses were required for the guidance of the traveller, which now, thanks to the wisdom of measures taken by their owners, present the best illustrations of fertility and productiveness.

"There are clayey tracts, which in some parts are a poverty-stricken dairy country, and in others, thanks to similar operations, are drained, tilled, and productive. On the one side, in these two pictures, we have a scanty population, earning a precarious livelihood, while on the other there are intelligence, activity, well-paid labour, well-supplied markets, and a prosperous tenantry.

"The difference between the two has been owing to the difference between energy and carelessness, between parsimony and liberality, between recklessness and wisdom, in the person and management of the landowner.

"The duties of a position on which so much depends are rarely performed in person, and thus the office of the land-agent or deputy, to whom they are very generally remitted, is one of very great importance.

"We do not know an estate on which the value of a wise and liberal and energetic superintendence has been more obviously proved than it has on the Northumberland property of the Greenwich Hospital. Nor is it, we believe, possible to name anyone to whom in this direct, local, and immediate manner English agriculture owes so much as it does to the gentleman whose name heads this paragraph, and who has now for more than thirty years administered this extensive property.

"Appointed so long ago as sole Superintendent of an Estate extending from Tweedmouth to Cross Fell, with all its vast mineral and agricultural productions, he might well feel diffident. He accepted the arduous post, however, and has since performed not only the mere duties of the office, but, in a most distinguished and public-spirited manner, those which every man in his position and degree owes to society. Mr. Grey, of Dilston, has been long-known as the great agricultural authority in the North of England, as the great promoter of agricultural improvement, as the founder of agricultural societies, as the heart and centre of every useful public movement in the agricultural world."

# CHAPTER VII

## THE GIRLS' MENFOLK AND PROGENY

ELIZA GREY – Mrs. WILLIAM MORRISON.

The eldest daughter of John and Hannah Grey was named Hannah Eliza after her mother but was known as Eliza in the family, no doubt to avoid confusion and this is how she is here referred to.

Eliza was born at Milfield Hill on 10 April 1819, the year of Queen Victoria's birth. Eliza's childhood was spent at Milfield Hill and she was already sixteen when the family moved to Dilston in 1835. She was married in the following year at the age of seventeen. Unlike her sisters, she did not attend a boarding-school.

Eliza was married in Corbridge Parish Church on 13 September 1836 to William Morrison, a surgeon, aged twenty-four. He was born on 12 June 1812 at Llanelly, Caernarvon, Wales. His medical work first brought him to Newcastle. In 1836 the Newcastle-on-Tyne School of Medicine was established and William Morrison was the first licensed lecturer in Anatomy and Physiology at the School, a position he held for five years.

After their marriage the Morrisons lived at Pelaw, which was then a village in the County of Durham but is now within the Newcastle boundary. This was convenient for Dr. Morrison, as he was then known, because of his appointment at the School of Medicine, but he also had an outside practice. Emily Grey, his sister-in-law, recalled going to stay with the Morrisons after the wedding of her sister, Mary Ann (Tully), to Edgar Garston in September 1842. She had happy memories of her brother-in-law's kindness. She accompanied him on his rounds to the pit villages and she was intrigued by a tall case in his study containing what he described as "a beautiful female skeleton". At the time Eliza Morrison was nursing her first-born child, Edith. Dr. Morrison used to take the ingredients of toffee to his study, make toffee on the fire in a saucepan with Emily's help and carry it up to Eliza. William Morrison was elected Fellow of the Royal College of Surgeons when that degree was first instituted. Subsequently, in 1843, the Morrisons moved to Penrith in Cumberland, where they remained until 1847. During this period they had three more children, William Llewelyn, Constance and Anna Mary. For their children's transport there was a small phaeton which was drawn by a Newfoundland dog called Niger, in harness with two ponies, Bobby and Eddie; they were spirited and needed no persuasion.

In 1847 Mr. Morrison, F.R.C.S. was offered by the Government of Hong Kong the post of Senior Surgeon of the Colony. In November of that year the Morrisons left with their children for Hong Kong with a view to Mr. Morrison taking up the appointment.

Death of Mr. Morrison F.R.C.S.

After nearly six years in Hong Kong William Morrison became seriously ill. He died on 13 October 1853 from an abscess on the liver, at the early age of forty-one, and was buried in Hong Kong. The funeral was attended by the Governor, the Chief Justice and the leading members of the Colony. The Hong Kong Register of 18 October 1853 paid this tribute to him:

"From his appointment his services met with entire and cordial approval of the local Government. To a very thorough knowledge of his profession, Mr. Morrison joined an ease and freedom of manner, a warmth of heart and amiability of disposition which endeared him to all who had the pleasure of his acquaintance. Mr. Morrison had a mind truly catholic: whatever his religion, whatever his creed, the man wanting his advice, freely and easily obtained it."

A local paper of 27 March 1854 reported that a very handsome subscription had been made among Mr. Morrison's friends, patients and the public for the purpose of erecting a monument over his grave and that it was in the course of being designed by Charles St. George Cleverly.

Before the illness and death of Mr. Morrison his services to the Roman Catholic Missionaries who found themselves compelled to leave their stations in the interior to seek medical relief and rest in the Colony, were brought to the notice of the Emperor of France. A letter dated 12 January 1855 was addressed to Mr. Morrison by the Ministry of Foreign Affairs in Paris. It read:

"I had the pleasure of informing His Majesty the Emperor of the devotion and unselfishness which you displayed in looking after the French community in Hong Kong and especially the members of the Catholic Missions. His Majesty would very much have liked to confer on you, as evidence of his high esteem, the decoration of his Imperial Order, The Legion of Honour, but since the law of your country prevents this distinction being accorded you, the Emperor has directed me to present to you, in his name, the medal which accompanies this letter."

The news of Mr. Morrison's death caused great sorrow to the Grey family. John Grey wrote to a good friend as follows:

"Yesterday's post brought me letters from Hong Kong with the sad information that when the mail left on the 11 October, a few hours or at most days, must, to all human appearance, put an end to the life which has been so valuable to many, and the loss of which was exciting such deep sorrow and sympathy in the colony. But our affliction does not end there. Our dear daughter, who for seven weeks had waited, watched, and nursed her husband by day and night, with short intervals of rest, leaving little for Chinese servants to do, is at last prostrated, though still clinging to his bed when not forced away by fainting. Theirs was no common attachment. His condition is hopeless, and hers at best precarious. She managed to send a few brief lines to her mother, saying that she had had a happy life through many trials; and expressed herself content to die if it pleased God to take her too, commending to Him and to our care her four children. We must now endure a painful state of suspense until another mail arrives. I do hope and pray that our dear daughter may yet be spared to bring her children home. But it is a fearful distance and journey to encounter in circumstances of such heavy trial and sickness. The loss of our dear Eliza would be dreadful to her poor children and to us all, for, besides natural affection she possesses a sweetness of disposition and a superiority of mental qualities which gained for her general love and admiration."

## The Second Marriage of Eliza Morrison.

In the event Eliza Morrison returned home with her four children. At some later date she married a Mr. Masson who lived in Northern Italy and she made her home there with him. Her eldest daughter, Edith, married Ludwig Leupold whose address was La Coroneta, Genoa. In 1864 the Leupolds were living at Villa Spinola, Sestri Di Ponenta, near Genoa. Harriet Meuricoffre visited her niece, Edith Leupold, there. In a letter to her sister, Fanny Smyttan, she described their meeting in colourful terms: "Edith's pretty, bright home, with its crimson carpets and blazing, generous coal fires, looked so very inviting, and her welcome was very sweet and affectionate. She came running from her room where she was dressing for tea, with a long, waving tail of splendid black hair down her back."

The Leupolds had a daughter, Marie, who married first, Sir Lepel Griffin and, after his death in 1908, Colonel C.H. Grey, D.S.O. (formerly Charles Hoare). The Griffins had two sons; the elder, Ronnie, had a daughter Josephine; the younger, Sir Cecil Griffin, had a distinguished career in India. He died in 1964 unmarried. By her second marriage Marie had a daughter, Iris Marie, born in 1911. In 1938 she married W.G. Hayter, now Sir William Hayter,

K.C.M.G., formerly Warden of New College, Oxford.

## MARY ANN GREY (TULLY) - Mrs. EDGAR GARSTON

Mary Ann Grey, who was known in the family as Tully, was the second daughter of John and Hannah Grey. She was born on 7 July 1821 at Milfield Hill and was fourteen when the Grey family moved to Dilston. On 21 September 1842, at the age of twenty-one she married Edgar Garston who was considerably older than her. After their marriage they moved to near Liverpool, where her husband was a merchant. His address was shown as 64 Rodney Street in Liverpool.

In 1847 Edgar Garston bought land in Aigburth, a parish in the township of Garston, which was then outside Liverpool's town boundary. Soon after he built a commodious house on it. Here he and his wife lived during their thirty years of married life and brought up their two children. In the Liverpool directory Garston was shown as merchant of The Mount, Aigburth and of 3, Romford Place.

In the Grey family Garston was esteemed as a kindly man, a genial host and a raconteur. He had the reputation of being a hero of the Greek War of Independence and he regaled the young with accounts of his adventures. This reputation was not undeserved. Garston's early life was colourful and of exceptional interest, as will be seen from a book by him published in 1842.

Edgar Garston was born in Chester. His father was Timothy Jay Garston of Chester, a prosperous merchant who was admitted a Freeman of the City in 1813. There is reason to believe that he was connected with the glove trade. Edgar Garston received a good education. He knew Greek and Latin and was widely read. In 1820 he was a Queen's Messenger and carried papers relating to the trial of Queen Caroline before the House of Lords on a charge of adultery brought by King George IV.

In 1825 Garston went out to Greece as a Volunteer to help the Greeks in their fight for independence from Turkey. This was over a year after Byron's death from illness at Missolonghi in April 1824. The total number of Philhellene Volunteers is estimated at twelve hundred by an eminent authority, William St.Clair, author of *That Greece Might Still be Free. The Philhellenes in the War of Independence*. O.U.P. 1972. The part played by British citizens in the movement was small compared with that by Italians, Germans and French. In 1822 a battalion of Philhellenes was recruited in Europe but there were few British among them. Byron's death in Missolonghi and the subsequent protracted siege caused the town to become the symbol of the Greek War of Independence and a focus of Philhellene feeling. In 1824 and 1825 there was renewed support in Europe

JOHN GREY, the author's great-grandfather.
From a portrait by G. Patten, A.R.A., July 1852.

DILSTON HALL.
Built in 1835, photograph circa 1880.

DILSTON HALL.
As it is today, photograph 1980.

NORTHUMBERLAND COUNTY MAP.
Engraved by Sidney Hall, published by
Chapman & Hall, 186 Strand. May 1831.

ST. ANDREW'S CHURCH, CORBRIDGE.

CHARLTON HALL. Fanny Smytan's home on marriage in 1848. From a sepia drawing by Josephine Butler.

JOSEPHINE BUTLER at Liverpool, circa 1866.

From a watercolour by Josephine Butler of her
drawing-room at Oxford, circa 1855.

The Butlers leaving Oxford in 1857.
A comic sketch by Harriet Grey.

FAMILY GROUP circa 1902.
owing author with his mother and EMILY THOMAS née
Grey, his grandmother.

for the movement, especially in Germany, France and Switzerland.

In 1825 Garston was not a member of any organised body, whether from Britain or elsewhere. The circumstances of his lone venture can be deduced from the Journal which he kept, an extract of which is recorded in his book of 1842, which had the cumbersome title of *Greece Revisited and Sketches in Lower Egypt in 1840 with Thirty-six Hours of a Campaign in Greece in 1825. An Extract from my Journal.* The publishers were Saunders & Otley, Conduit Street, London. Garston wrote at the end of his book: "The sketch of the incidents of Thirty-six Hours in Greece in 1825 is added as bringing into view some of those who are named in the Journal."

Garston described himself as an English Philhellene. It is not clear whether he had any backing other than letters of introduction, but it would seem that he first went to the Ionian Islands on the west coast of Greece which had in 1815 been taken under protection by Britain and were under a High Commissioner. Garston was conveyed to Hydra, an island off the east coast of Greece, which was a naval base for Greek and British ships. At Hydra he was fitted out with the dress worn by Greek irregular volunteers, who were known as Pellekars. In Greek "Pellekari" meant literally "a young man" but had acquired the meaning of "a brave man". Pellekaria, anglicised as "Pellekars", was the name given to irregular soldiery to distinguish them from regular troops such as the force formed in Athens in 1826 by a distinguished Frenchman, Colonel Fabvier. The dress worn by the Pellekars was the native costume of Greek and Albanian mountaineers consisting of an embroidered jacket and white linen kilt, with a swathed skull-cap for headgear. Christian Albanians, known as Suliotes, formed the backbone of the irregular troops. Garston's book carried a picture of a Suliote Pellekar in his picturesque native costume complete with scimitar.

From Hydra Garston went to Nauplia, the seat of the Provisional Greek Government at the head of the Gulf of Nauplia. Here he was given a letter of introduction to the Greek Commander of the irregulars in Morea, the renowned Theodore Colccotronis, described as the most formidable of Greek local war-lords, and to a General Botsaris. This letter, dated 24 August 1825, was signed by the President of Greece, George Conduriottis, who was a Hydriote ship-owner, and by Alexander Mavrocordato, the Secretary-General. The letter read as follows:

"PROVISIONAL GOVERNMENT OF GREECE.
THE EXECUTIVE BODY.

To the very brave General Constantine Botsaris.

The English Philhellene, Mr. Edgar Garston, who is the bearer of the present, comes to you in order to travel through and examine certain parts of Eastern Greece, and also that he may become acquainted with the army (or camp) in that quarter. You are instructed therefore to receive him with distinguished welcome and protection, facilitating to him the means of accomplishing his object according to his desires.

Nauplia, 24 August 1825.
                    The Secretary-General,
The President,          A. Mavrocordato.
    George Conduriottis.                    "

Garston crossed to the Morea and reported to Colocotronis. He was assigned to a unit of irregulars from Cephalonia, one of the Ionian Islands. With them he took part in a battle at Tricorfa, or "Three Plateaux", in the mountains above the Turkish stronghold of Tripolitsa. The tactics employed by the Pellekars were to build breastworks of stones and earth, called tambouria, which afforded them cover, especially when loading their muskets. Garston recalled how persistent attacks by a Turkish force composed of Turkish cavalry and Egyptian infantry were repelled. He observed that the "Arab Infantry" were clothed in dark brown material and their officers in very dark crimson uniforms, which gave them rather

59

a thunder-cloud aspect when seen at a distance. It was claimed that this was the first occasion on which Pellekar Irregulars had got the better of Turkish regular troops.

During operations in the mountains Garston was attached to the Commander, Theodore Colocotronis, messing with him and his officers, sitting cross-legged at a low table and eating out of the same dish. Garston, who was a pipe smoker, used a chibouque or Turkish tobacco-pipe with amber mouthpiece and long wooden stem. Pipe smoking accompanied by coffee drinking together with companions was a ritual among the Greeks who smoked a Syrian weed as an opiate of pain and anxiety. Garston was assigned his own pipe carrier or chibouquee.

In these rough conditions it is hardly surprising that Garston contracted dysentery. This necessitated his being carried on a stretcher to hospital at Vervena, and thus ended the thirty-six hours depicted by him as the most stirring in his service with the Moreot forces. After his recovery Garston joined the Greek naval forces at Hydra. This island had a population of about twenty thousand, of whom four to five thousand were seamen. Its inhabitants, who were of Albanian origin although Greek-speaking, were renowned for their skill as ship-builders. The greater part of the Greek fleet of ninety vessels consisted of schooners and brigs of ten or twelve guns which had been built at Hydra.

Garston served as a volunteer on the Epaminondas, an eighteen-gun brig commanded by Captain Antonio G. Kriezis, a Hydriote of Albanian extraction. On this ship Garston took part in various naval operations. The Epaminondas was one of a fleet of small ships under the command of Admiral Canaris which made an unsuccessful attempt to set fire to ships of the Egyptian fleet anchored in Alexandria harbour. Garston then suffered from an attack of fever of the kind which proved fatal to many of his countrymen and he stayed on a British naval vessel during his convalescence. Soon after returning to duty he was compelled by a similar fever to quit Greece in 1826. He left Hydra for home on a British frigate, H.M.S. Seringapatam.

The major portion of Garston's book, each volume of which is over three hundred pages, is devoted to a description of his visit to Greece in 1840, fourteen years after he had been evacuated from it. In his Preface he wrote that circumstances had thrown him into constant and intimate association with the leading Moreot Chiefs, with the members of the Provisional Government and with the most distinguished of those gallant invaders who had earned for themselves an undying name in the marine "guerilla" warfare which was waged by their tiny vessels with the leviathans of the Porte (Turkey). In the Preface Garston said only that circumstances had induced him to turn his steps towards the scenes of his earlier experiences but did not state what those circumstances were. It is clear, however, that a principal aim was to establish contact with Pellekars of the old school who had been his companions in arms in Morea in 1825. Among those with whom he established contact in 1840 were his old commander, Theodore Colocotronis, and the commander of the brig Epaminondas, Antonio G. Kriezis, who had by now become Minister of Marine.

In 1840 Greece was a monarchy. Otto, son of King Ludwig of Bavaria, had ascended the throne in 1833 at the early age of seventeen. On 8 March 1840 there was a ball at the Palace to which Garston was invited. He was presented to King Otto and his beautiful consort, both of whom were in Albanian national costume. On 1 April 1840 Garston had, to quote from his Journal, "the gratification of receiving through the office of the Minister of Marine, the Silver National Cross of Merit". This Cross was conferred only on those who had seen active service during the War of Independence and was for that reason more prized than the Cross of the Saviour. There were three grades – Iron, Bronze and Silver – which were bestowed according to the rank or services of him on whom it was conferred. Subsequently Garston was received in private audience by King Otto.

On the title-page of both volumes of his book Garston is shown as "Knight of the R.M. Greek Order of the Saviour etc.," but in his book he does not enlarge on the bestowal of this decoration. William St.Clair, in his work on the Greek War of Independence, which was referred to earlier, says that in 1829 the Greek Provisional Government planned to confer the Order of the Saviour on all Philhellenes who had taken part in the War and to record their names in a Book of Remembrance. But the promised lists were not drawn up and soon the names of many of the Philhellenes were forgotten. In May 1841 a few former Philhellenes gathered at Nauplia for the dedication of a simple monument on the columns of which were inscribed the names of two hundred and seventy-eight Philhellenes who were known to have been killed in the War of Independence or died in Greece in the course of it. Garston's return to Greece in 1840 seems to have been animated by a similar wish – to pay a tribute to former participants in the War of Independence.

A considerable portion of the first volume of Garston's book is taken up by a description of famous ruins in Greece. He knew classical Greek and was knowledgeable in archaeology. This and his love of travel were his reasons for visiting Lower Egypt later in 1840. A chapter on Egypt in the second volume is entitled Present Conditions in Egypt. Garston made a study of the administration of the country by the Viceroy of the

Sultan of Turkey in Egypt, Mohammed Ali Pasha, who had earlier seized the Sudan in the name of Turkey. Garston estimated the strength of the naval and military forces of Egypt and Turkey against the background of the continuing rivalry between Turkey and certain Christian European Powers. His detailed assessment is set out in two Appendices but there is no indication for whom the data were intended.

Garston inscribed his book to his father as a testimony of veneration and affection. This book was published after some delay in 1842, the year of his marriage to Mary Ann Grey. Members of her family were vaguely acquainted with Garston's exploits but the book was not referred to in family correspondence, as far as is known, and only a lucky chance led to it being known by, and made available to, the author of this study. For this he is much indebted to Mr. William St.Clair, Fellow of All Souls College, Oxford, whose masterly work on the Greek War of Independence was noted earlier. A copy of Garston's book, dated 1845, is to be found in the Council Library, Montrose.

Garston's visit to Greece in 1840 was only an interlude in his business career. He had engaged in business in Liverpool as early as 1832, although retaining his connection with Chester. In 1857 he presented four drinking fountains to Chester and followed this up with a further four. Only one of these fountains survives. It is situated by Watergate Bridge at the western entrance to the city. It carries the same inscription as did the other fountains: The Gift of E.G., K.S. 1857.

Members of the Garston family are today planning to repair this fountain. Their uncertainty as to the significance of K S has been dispelled by the evidence of Garston's book. On the title-page of both volumes Garston is shown as "Knight of the R M Greek Order of the Saviour etc.,". K S on the fountain undoubtedly indicated his membership of this Order, of which he was very proud.

Edgar Garston and his wife had two children. The first-born was Ethel, born in 1853, eleven years after her parents' marriage. Their son, Edgar, was born in 1856 and baptised in St. Anne's Church, Aigburth on 9 August 1856. In 1875 Ethel Garston, then aged twenty-three, married Francis John Budd aged twenty-eight, a bachelor, merchant and resident of Liverpool, son of James Budd, merchant. The marriage was by licence and was conducted by the Reverend George Butler, her uncle.

Edgar Garston lived to be nearly eighty. In 1880, soon after Edgar Garston's death, Harriet Meuricoffre and her husband visited England. She wrote to her son in Naples describing the visit paid by herself and two sisters to "the dear Mount where Tully Garston had spent thirty peaceful years of her married life". The four sisters, Tully,

Fanny, Josephine and Hatty, went to Aigburth church which "Tully had attended with her husband for thirty years". Hatty recalled Edgar's fine sonorous voice. The sermon was preached by Josephine's husband, the Reverend George Butler. After church the party returned to Liverpool where the three sisters were staying with Josephine Butler and her husband who was then Principal of Liverpool College and nearing retirement.

The Mount still stands in Aigburth, now a residential suburb of Liverpool, at the junction of Elmswood Road and Woodlands Road. Some years ago the top of the house was destroyed by fire but the main portion containing the ballroom survived.

Mr. Budd predeceased his wife, Ethel, who was left comfortably off. Towards the end of her life she lived in North Oxford, in number 8, Chadlington Road, where she entertained numerous relations. When the author was an undergraduate, from 1919–1922, he enjoyed her hospitality and the opportunity of meeting distant cousins and also members of the academic world, including Julian Huxley. Among the cousins were Cecil Griffin, who is referred to earlier in this study, and Gwendolen Garston, daughter of Edgar Garston junior and his wife, Maud Carter. Miss E. Moberly Bell, author of *Josephine Butler. A Biography*, in her author's note thanked Miss Gwendolen Garston for "guidance about illustrations and family memories".

FRANCES HARDY GREY (FANNY) – Mrs. GEORGE HUNT SMYTTAN

Frances, generally known as Fanny, was born on 28 May 1823. She was two years younger than Mary Ann and five years older than Josephine. When the Grey family moved to Dilston she was twelve and she spent thirteen years there until her marriage to the Reverend G.H. Smyttan in St. Andrew's, Corbridge on 15 June 1848, at the age of twenty-five.

G.H. Smyttan was born in 1822 and was therefore a year older than Fanny. He was the son of George Hunt Smyttan M.D. of the Bombay Medical Board. The marriage certificate described G.H. Smyttan junior as Esquire and gave his address as Charlton Hall, Ellingham. Charlton Hall is in the parish of Ellingham-with-Charlton, some miles north-west of Alnwick.

It is known that George Smyttan entered Corpus Christi College, Cambridge in 1843 and achieved his B.A. in 1848. Records in Church House, Dean's Yard, Westminster show that he was ordained Deacon in Durham on 1 July 1848, that is to say within a fortnight of his marriage. Family records state that he had a living between Falloden and Hawick but do not specify the parish.

The Church House records show that he was curate of Ellingham-with-Alnwick, Northumberland, from 1848 to 1850 and that in 1849 he was a priest. They also show him as Rector of Hawksworth in Nottinghamshire from 1850 to 1859 and as having achieved his M.A. at Corpus Christi College, Cambridge in 1859. He is shown as "Author of Mission Songs and Ballads and several well-known hymns including 'Forty Days and Forty Nights'." In 1859 he received an M.A. degree, presumably honorary, at Oxford. In 1860 his name no longer appeared in Crockford's Clerical Directory. The last entry in the Clergy House Record is "Died suddenly at Frankfurt-on-Main, 21 February 1870 (aged 48)."

As far as family records are concerned, there is scarcely any reference to Fanny's family life and, such references as there are, are not consistent with the records quoted above.

Fanny was very talented. She was a star pupil at school and had real artistic talent. Two albums of her drawings are available. One is dated 15 August 1837 and contains pencil drawings initialled F.H.G. The other has inscribed at the front "Fanny Grey, Dilston, 1848", the year of her marriage. The latter album contains sepia drawings of which twenty-seven are initialled F.H.S. (i.e., Frances Hardy Smyttan). This album also contains some sketches by Josephine Butler initialled at the foot in her familiar violet ink. Among them is a sepia drawing of a substantial house inscribed in Josephine Butler's own writing "Charlton Hall. Aunt Fanny's first home when she married". In her

68

*Recollections* Emily Grey tells how she stayed with her sister Fanny near Alnwick, without specifying the name of the place.

In correspondence between the Grey sisters a few references suggest that she was delicate and to be pitied. For instance, Josephine wrote in a letter to her grandson, "Poor Aunt Fanny. You can see from her sketch-book that had she had advantages such as people have nowadays, and a stronger hand, she would have been a real artist."

Fanny was a frequent visitor at Dilston in times of trouble. After the death of her mother in 1860 she took over the running of the household and she looked after her father until his death in 1868. She moved to Lipwood House with him in 1863 and accompanied him on a journey abroad to stay with his daughter, Harriet Meuricoffre. John Grey wrote to a granddaughter, Edith Leupold, on 5 September 1863: "You have had a description of this our new residence from Fanny who has been indefatigable in arranging and settling all things with taste and judgment." Harriet wrote to Fanny in 1864, "what good service you have done to the dear Butler family when they were in such sorrow (1864) and with little Stanley so near death".

Soon after the Rev. George Butler and his wife had moved to Liverpool in 1866, Josephine became interested in helping girls who were working on the quays and in oakum sheds. She wrote inviting Fanny to join her and help in the work. To quote the words of Miss E. Moberly Bell in her biography of Josephine Butler: "Josephine wrote to her sister Fanny, recently widowed and suggested she should come to help her. Fanny responded with alacrity and threw herself whole-heartedly into the work." A workroom was obtained and the girls flocked to it and worked with such zeal that Josephine and her sister were hard put to it to keep them supplied with materials. The girls had to be fitted out with a suitable wardrobe after which Fanny would escort them to their new home (a Rescue Home). Miss Bell was at fault in describing Fanny as "recently widowed" seeing that her husband died in 1870.

There is no hint in correspondence of the 1860s as to where the Rev. George Smyttan was or as to the relationship between him and Fanny. In connection with her mother's death, Josephine Butler wrote in her *Memoir* of her father that a compensation for him for his bereavement in 1860 was the return to his home of one of his children, the faithful daughter who was destined to be the companion of his declining years. It must be remembered that John Grey died in 1868 and that Fanny's husband was still alive then.

Somewhat surprisingly Fanny lived to be seventy-two. Josephine Butler quoted in her book *In Memoriam – Harriet Meuricoffre* from an item in her own journal written at Gordanne, Switzerland in September 1895: "We received this month the news of the death of our dear sister Fanny, after many years of lonely childless widowhood and much physical pain and weakness. We were sad, yet glad, that she is at peace, her 'warfare accomplished'."

The hiatus in the clerical records between 1860 and 1870 is unexplained. The Librarian of Corpus Christi College, Cambridge informed the author that he had not found that G.H. Smyttan had won any prizes or was otherwise prominent in College affairs.

What took G.H. Smyttan to Germany in 1870 and what led to his sudden death at the comparatively early age of forty-eight is likely to remain a mystery. It is always possible that the answer may be found by someone specialising in the lives of hymn-writers.


JOSEPHINE ELIZABETH GREY - Mrs. GEORGE BUTLER

Josephine Grey was the fourth of the six daughters of John and Hannah Grey, whose upbringing of their large family, first at Milfield Hill and later at Dilston Hall, is described in earlier chapters. She was born on 15 April 1828.

Josephine was thirteen years younger than her eldest brother, George, and nine years younger than Eliza, her eldest sister. There was a gap of five years between herself and her elder sister, Fanny, but only two years between herself and her younger sister, Hatty.

71

Emily, the youngest daughter, was eight years her junior and very much the baby of the family. It was therefore natural that Josephine and Hatty should have paired off at Dilston Hall and they maintained a close relationship throughout their lives. Josephine wrote a book about Hatty *In Memoriam: Harriet Meuricoffre*, which she dedicated to Harriet's children and grandchildren. It was written and published within a year of Harriet's death in 1900 or 1901.

Josephine was aged seven when the family moved to the newly-built house at Dilston in 1835 and she spent seventeen years there before her marriage in 1852 when aged twenty-four. Josephine became acquainted with her future husband, George Butler, in 1851 when he was a tutor at Durham University. He belonged to a family which was distinguished for its scholarship. George Butler (1819-1890) was the eldest of the four sons of George Butler (1774-1853) who was Headmaster of Harrow School and later Dean of Peterborough. Two others of George Butler's four sons also distinguished themselves in the teaching profession, becoming, respectively, Headmaster of Harrow School and, Headmaster of Haileybury College in its early years.

Josephine and George Butler were married in Corbridge Parish Church on 8 January 1852. After their marriage they lived at Oxford as George Butler was public examiner at Oxford University and was later appointed Lecturer in

Geography, which he helped to establish as a major subject. At Oxford, when they lived at 124, High St., the Butlers had a wide circle of friends in the academic world. They entertained their friends at musical evenings which afforded Josephine the opportunity of performing on her magnificent Broadwood pianoforte. It features in an admirable watercolour by Josephine of a drawing-room at Oxford, which is contained in a sketch-book, now with the author.

In 1853 George Butler took orders in the Church of England, being ordained by Bishop Wilberforce. He felt that the teaching profession was his vocation and that he would be better equipped for teaching if he was in the Church.

He was eminently suited for the teaching profession. He was at Harrow School and Exeter College, Oxford where he was a Scholar. He graduated with First Class Honours in Classics and in 1842 was elected a Fellow of Exeter. He was a good linguist, a fine athlete and artistic. He was also a mountaineer and he combined sketching landscapes in watercolour with mountaineering.

During the period at Oxford three sons were born to the Butlers: George Grey (15 November 1852); Arthur Stanley (17 May 1854) and Charles Augustine Vaughan (16 May 1856). The Oxford climate turned out to be detrimental to Josephine's health and she was advised by her doctors to make a change. The opportunity came when in 1857 the Rev.

George Butler was offered the post of Vice-Principal of Cheltenham College which he accepted. The time at Cheltenham College began happily. A daughter, Evangeline, was born in 1858 and the Butlers had many outside interests, especially in The American Civil War, and in the abolition of slavery, their views on which came into conflict with those prevailing in Cheltenham society.

The Butlers' life was, however, disrupted by the tragic death in August 1864 of their six years old daughter, Evangeline, who fell over banisters when running from her upstairs room to greet her parents on their return from an evening function.

Providentially, the Rev. George Butler was invited to become Principal of Liverpool College, which he accepted in 1865. It had been known as Liverpool Collegiate Institution, having been formed on the basis of an Upper and Middle School, but its name had been changed in 1864. There had been two Principals only, William John Conybeare and the Rev. J.S. Houson, who resigned after seventeen years in 1865. In the course of seventeen years the Rev. George Butler reorganised the College and greatly increased its academic reputation, especially in the field of Geography. He had been faced with a dilemma: to make the school pay or to make it a forcing-house to a university education, and he chose the latter course. His three sons made their mark at the school. In later life the eldest, George Grey Butler F.R.G.S., F.G.S., was a permanent examiner to the Civil Service Commission and a member of the Council of Durham University. Arthur Stanley Butler became Professor of Natural Philosophy at St.Andrew's University. Information about Liverpool College has been derived from a book entitled, *Liverpool Gentlemen. A History of Liverpool College* by David Wainwright and published in 1960 by Faber & Faber Ltd, 24 Russell Square, London W.C.1.

Josephine Butler's Campaign for Social Reform.

Josephine Butler found at Liverpool an outlet for her aspiration to elevate the status of women. In 1869 she began to campaign for the repeal of the Contagious Diseases Act, which she believed degraded women by putting responsibility for prostitution on girls who were the victims of their social conditions. In a campaign which took her up and down the country in 1869 and later into Europe, the Butlers' house was a headquarters for her work. The Rev. George Butler gave her his loyal support but he could not enjoy the well-ordered life of the Principal of a College and he incurred criticism from his detractors for his open support of his wife's campaign.

In March 1882 the Rev. George Butler resigned the post of Principal and in June he was nominated by the Prime

Minister, William Ewart Gladstone, to a Canonry of Winchester Cathedral. Soon Josephine Butler's campaign drew to a triumphant conclusion and George Butler enjoyed eight restful years at Winchester which were broken only by some holidays abroad. He died in 1898 aged seventy-one. The reader is referred to the book, mentioned in the earlier paragraph, which describes the personality and academic distinction of the Rev. George Butler very well.

In her widowhood Josephine Butler greatly enjoyed the companionship of her sons, George Grey and Arthur Stanley and their children. George Grey Butler and his wife, Maria, daughter of Sir Horace St.Paul, had three children. Arthur Stanley Butler married his first cousin, Rhoda, daughter of Jasper Bolton and his wife Emily (née Grey) Arthur Stanley and Rhoda Butler had two children: A.S.G. Butler (known in the family as Andrew) and a daughter Josephine, named after her grandmother. Josephine found a special pleasure in the company of these two grandchildren, Andrew and Josephine, who were also the grandchildren of her sister, Emily, with whom she kept in touch at the same time.

A Holiday in Switzerland.

A.S.G. Butler in his book *Portrait of Josephine Butler* referred to the voluminous correspondence which she conducted with him and his sister when they were children, in the decade 1895 to

1905. Many of these letters survived. There is also a reference by him to a special occasion in the summer of 1899 when Josephine Butler took the four members of the Butler family to Switzerland on a holiday. The account of the holiday in diary form is contained in a foolscap book entitled *Our Swiss Journey*. It comprises forty written pages and thirty-five pages of sketches, scenic photographs and small pictures. The diary, beginning at Berne on 1 August and ending at Cologne on 18 September 1899, was written by Josephine Butler in her familiar purple ink. She used the first person plural, we, purporting to speak for all five members of the party who are mentioned by name as the occasion required: Granny (J.E.B.), Daddy (Stanley Butler), Mother (Rhoda Butler), Josephine and Andrew. Stanley Butler, being a skilful mountaineer, introduced the two children to the joys of mountaineering. The party travelled home via the Rhine Valley. This diary, now with the author, is a remarkable feat, bearing in mind that Josephine Butler was then in her seventy-first year.

Towards the end of her life, Josephine Butler lived at Wooler, a town in Northumberland in Glendale Ward, which she had known well as a child since her old home, Milfield Hill, was near it. She died on 30 December 1906 aged seventy-eight. She was buried in the churchyard of Kirknewton, a few miles from Wooler.

So much has been written by and

about Josephine Butler that any attempt by the author to assess her life's work would be inadequate and might be misleading. Her grandson, Andrew Butler, was eighteen when she died and was in a position to describe her complex character, which he did in his *Portrait of Josephine Butler*, published in 1954. He shows how her love of justice and hatred of injustice forced her to campaign for social causes and that she was generous to a degree, loved children and animals and had intense religous conviction, amounting to mysticism. He thought that her greatest traits were her humility and her spell-binding oratory. She was a compulsive letter-writer, her literary output was prodigious, and a great deal was written about her, as will be seen from sources quoted by Miss E. Moberly Bell in her biography: *Josephine Butler. Flame of Fire*.

Josephine Butler wrote about herself that "when a girl at Dilston she felt the burden of inequality, injustice and cruelty in the world to be so great that she used to run into the woods and shout to God for deliverance". She suspected that her sisters thought her a little mad. If they did so at the time, there is certainly no trace of this in correspondence exchanged with them in later years; instead the correspondence shows that they had great affection for her and greatly respected her unusual talents and dedication. Her memory dimmed over the years but interest in her work has been resuscitated by feminist movements in a number of countries, including Germany and the United States.

Josephine Butler Remembered in the Alternative Service Book 1980.

The Synod of the Church of England, in 1978, included her among those who are remembered in the Alternative Service Book together with the Liturgical Psalter, which was published in 1980. Lesser Festivals and Commemorations are listed in its Calendar: against 30 December is written "Josephine Butler, Social Reformer. Wife. Mother. 1907."

HARRIET JANE GREY (HATTY) – Mme. TELL MEURICOFFRE

Harriet, who was known in the Grey family as Hatty, was the fifth of the six daughters of John and Hannah Grey. She was born on 18 April 1830. There was a gap of only two years between her and Josephine and a much bigger gap between her and Fanny and it was inevitable that she and Josephine should pair off in their early years. They were at school together as boarders for two years and they were married within two years of one another. Throughout their long lives, although separated by distance, they kept in constant touch and met periodically.

Josephine survived Hatty by five years and her book entitled *In Memoriam - Harriet Meuricoffre* was dedicated to the latter's children and grandchildren. It was published by Horace Marshall & Son in 1901, only a year after Hatty's death. It is full of information about Hatty's long married life which, to quote from the book, "was one of many and varied interests, a very full life shadowed by storms, yet, as she herself loved to acknowledge, with many and rare blessings". The book comprises a selection from correspondence between the sisters, with comments describing the context of the letters.

Harriet is believed to have met her future husband, Tell Meuricoffre, when he visited England on his way back from a business journey to the United States. He was Swiss by birth but lived most of his life in Naples. He was a banker, a member of a prosperous banking concern. He was sturdy, a mountaineer and a lover of the countryside. He was also an accomplished pianist and had a talent for sketching. He was a Protestant and played an active part in the Protestant community in Naples for many years.

Harriet married Tell Meuricoffre in Corbridge Parish Church on 24 August 1854 at the age of twenty-four. She left Dilston Hall, where she had lived from the age of five, to accompany her husband to his home in Southern Italy. They broke the journey in Paris staying with Tell's relations. Harriet wrote home to say that they had seen everything there of interest, with her husband acting as guide as he had lived in Paris for some years studying with a distinguished tutor.

Harriet's wedding present from her father consisted of his two favourite horses, Dilston and Una. They reached Paris safely in a horse-box and were brought into use there and then. They attracted the attention of a party of ladies, dressed in fine bonnets, feathers and flounces, who came to see them unloaded. When Una was brought out she was patted by the ladies with their primrose and lavender kid gloves; she slavered her nose over velvet mantles and cashmere shawls and looked pleased about it.

Harriet was enchanted by her husband's house, Villa Meuricoffre, Cape di Monte, Naples. She described it as very beautiful, overlooking the Bay of Naples, with the Appenines in the distance. It was in the country, surrounded by cornfields, vineyards and woods suited for quiet rides. She depicted her husband's working day: "he left home before seven and worked until four in the afternoon, returning by five for dinner." They would ride between seven and ten while it was still daylight.

The early years passed tranquilly enabling Harriet to visit her parents in England but the political situation deteriorated, following the death of Bomba, the aged Bourbon King of the Two Sicilies. There was strong opposition to the young King, Francis II (1859-61) because of the excessive power of the police. The Meuricoffres were shown the grim prison in the Fortress of St. Elmo, which, under the Bourbons, had been filled by patriots.

## Garibaldi and his Red Shirts.

The House of Savoy based on Sardinia had been in contention with Austria over Italy. Victor Emmanuel, with the assistance of France, defeated the Austrians in 1859 and by 1860 most of Italy was under his rule but his plan for a united Italy was blocked by the Bourbon Kingdom of the Two Sicilies (Sicily and Naples). There was open war between the supporters of the Bourbons and an army of Red Shirt Volunteers led by Garibaldi. The Royalists were defeated and Sicily and Naples were merged in the new Kingdom of Italy.

Preceding Garibaldi's entry into Naples in September 1860 there was a fierce engagement at Caserta, in which an English Brigade of five hundred had participated. There was a large number of wounded and Sophie, wife of Oscar Meuricoffre, Tell's elder brother, had taken over a ward of wounded in the Jesuit hospital. She was joined by Harriet and they had at their disposal money subscribed by English ladies.

The Meuricoffres were invited to call on Garibaldi at his Headquarters at Caserta. He was in the Palace but occupied three rooms only. His personal attendant was a monk, wearing a sword and top boots under his brown robe.

Garibaldi was writing at a desk with a quill pen in a fine bold hand, but he greeted his visitors warmly, shaking hands in a simple, unaffected way. Harriet was greatly impressed by Garibaldi, and thought that his one fault was that he was too guileless for this world. She thought that Garibaldi had worked a kind of regeneration in the outlook of the Neapolitans. The Meuricoffres were also invited to the Ceremonial Consecration of King Victor Emmanuel. They thought him ugly, with ferocious eyes, but with a frank bearing and appreciative of the duties of a constitutional monarch.

The Meuricoffres had the means to raise a considerable family and to exchange visits with their English relations. Their first-born was a daughter, Thekla, followed by three sons, Fred, George and Conrad, and lastly two little girls, Beatrice and Josephine. The Meuricoffres had a house in Switzerland to which they could retire in the heat of the summer, named La Gordanne, in the Canton Vaud. Its grounds were on the shore of Lake Geneva. In 1864 John Grey and his daughter Fanny stayed there.

In the autumn of 1865 there was an epidemic of cholera in Naples. Beatrice, a beautiful and happy child, contracted cholera and died. In 1866, when the Meuricoffres were in England on a visit, taking with them their baby girl Josephine, she died, having ceased to thrive after losing her sister.

When on their way to England, the Meuricoffres passed through Milan when Italy was on the brink of war. Milan Cathedral was full of Italian soldiers seeking a blessing in advance of an imminent battle against the Austrians. The Austrians won the Battle of Custozza but, following Prussia's victory over Austria at Sadowa in Czechoslovakia on 3 July 1866, Venice was acquired by Italy, thus completing the unification of Italy under King Victor Emmanuel.

The Meuricoffres were witnesses of yet further upheavals. On 24 April 1872 Vesuvius erupted. The mountain vomited smoke and ashes for three days leaving Naples covered with ash resembling grains of iron and causing smarting of the skin. In 1883 there was a terrible earthquake on the Island of Ischia, in the Bay of Naples. The whole Meuricoffre family took part in working to relieve the survivors.

In 1884 cholera broke out in Naples. Harriet was in England with the two younger sons, George and Conrad. Leaving them at school in England, she returned to Naples where her sister-in-law, Sophie Meuricoffre, was running a soup kitchen. Harriet worked for six weeks in the Hospital della Madellena, helping the nuns to nurse the sick. In 1885 Josephine Butler and her husband visited Naples and were shown the International Hospital which Tell Meuricoffre had founded and of which he was the first President; also the Sailors'

Rest, which Harriet had supported from its foundation.

In 1886 Thekla, the Meuricoffre's surviving daughter, married a Swiss gentleman, Henri Neher, who was an advocate in Egypt. In 1888 Harriet went to stay with her daughter. She went out in a crowded ship but returned on the S.S. Liguria, which was under the management of Thomas Cook, and was the only first-class passenger. Harriet was met by the Nehers in their carriage, M. Neher driving his capering little horses and a fleet-footed groom with a melodious voice running in front to clear the way. Hatty's description of life in Egypt was apt and the country had a fascination for her but she deplored the lowly status of Egyptian women.

In 1892 the Meuricoffres lost their youngest son Conrad who died of yellow fever in Rio de Janiero where he was engaged in work connected with banking. In March 1900 Tell Meuricoffre died in Naples and Hatty died within a year of him. An obituary in a Naples paper said that as head and support of the Swiss Protestant colony he was the promoter of countless good works. Truth, purity, uprightness, single-mindedness and munificent generosity were among his characteristics. Besides his public acts of benevolence he aided privately numbers of individuals and families whose needs he kept a secret.

Harriet spent her last days at her Swiss home. On her way she stayed with

Mrs. Masson, the former Mrs. William
Morrison, "our dear and venerable elder
sister", as Josephine Butler described
her. Harriet also stayed at Zurich with
Mme. Neher, her daughter Thekla's
mother-in-law. In her last letters she
wrote of her long partnership with Tell,
with its many blessings. She was buried
in the cemetery adjoining the grounds of
her beloved Gordanne, on the shore of
Lake Geneva.


EMILY GEORGINA GREY - Mrs. WILLIAM De
                      PLEDGE
                      Mrs. JASPER BOLTON
                      Mrs. F.W. THOMAS


Emily Georgina, the youngest of the
six Grey girls, was born at Dilston Hall
on 27 May 1836. She was much the
youngest, there being a six-year gap
between her and Harriet (Hatty). She was
a lonely child as her mother was
preoccupied with the affairs of a large
household in entirely new surroundings,
the move to Dilston having been effected
in 1835, and she was entrusted as a
child to a nursemaid and subsequently to
a nursery governess. In her
Recollections, written early in the present
century, Emily described herself as
somewhat rebellious, not very successful
at her boarding school and too much of a
handful for a governess at home. There
was, however, another side to her
nature, to judge from her own description

of herself; she was devoted to animals and the countryside, had a retentive and enquiring mind and unusual powers of observation. She was capable of great devotion. This was more evident in her relations with men than women, witness her love for her father and her brothers John and Charles, but she did not wear her feelings on her sleeve.

Emily's life was a most unusual one. She was three times married and survived all three husbands. In 1856, when aged only twenty, she married William De Pledge of Gateshead, by whom she had three children, two boys and a girl. De Pledge died in 1860. Within two years Emily married Jasper Bolton who was five years her junior. The marriage was registered in Pembroke district in 1862.

Jasper Bolton was brother-in-law to Emily De Pledge. To understand this relationship one has to note how the Boltons and Greys first came to be connected.

A certain Thomas Bolton (1797-1853) was the eldest son of William Bolton of The Mountain, Whittingham in Northumberland and his wife Elizabeth, a member of the Vardy family, which also came from Whittingham and was connected with the Grey family. Thomas Bolton was land-agent to Lord Derby for his Irish Estates and he lived in Ballykisteen, a large house on the property near Cullen in County Tipperary. On 29 June 1833 he married Eliza Bell (1800-1867). She was a member of a Quaker family, the Bells, who were closely linked with the Barclays and Gurneys of Norfolk. The marriage took place in England but the first child of the marriage, Emily Mary, was born in Ireland in October 1834, her birth being registered in the Baptismal Register of Cullen Church on 20 October 1834. The couple had five more children, all of whom were born in Ireland. Their fifth child was named Jasper Bolton (1841–1871). He married Emily De Pledge in 1862, as stated earlier.

In 1853 Emily Mary, daughter of Thomas Bolton, married Charles Grey (1825–1915) the youngest son of John and Hannah Grey of Dilston and elder brother of Emily Grey. She was then nineteen years old and he was twenty–eight. In the summer of 1853 a party including Charles Grey, Emily Mary Bolton and Harriet Grey had visited south–west Ireland and explored the Mangerton Mountain which lies between Killarney and Bantry Bay. The expedition was described by Harriet and it appears that Charles and Emily Mary had been married earlier in that year, so this may have been their honeymoon.

Thomas Bolton died in 1853 and was succeeded in the post of agent for Lord Derby's Irish Estates by Charles Grey who belonged to the Irish Land Commission and was a Justice of the Peace for Tipperary County. Charles Grey moved into Ballykisteen House with his wife Emily Mary. They had three children: Oswald (12 August 1854); Hilda

(3 August 1856) and Ralph born in 1862. Oswald died at Cullen in 1856 and Hilda died at Dilston in 1863. Ralph lived to a ripe old age.

In 1862 Charles Grey relinquished the post of land-agent to Lord Derby and in 1863 took over the post of Receiver for the Greenwich Hospital Estates from his father John Grey on the latter's retirement.

## Jasper Bolton in Ireland.

Jasper Bolton, at the time of his marriage to Emily De Pledge, was living at Sandymount, near Ballykisteen. He succeeded his brother-in-law, Charles Grey, as agent to Lord Derby and moved into Ballykisteen House on its vacation by Charles Grey. In due course Emily Georgina had five children by him. The eldest, Edith Rhoda, was born at Sandymount on 20 November 1862. Three children were born at Ballykisteen House: Thomas in 1863, Constance in 1866 and Arthur William (the author's father) in 1868. The youngest child Ruth was born in Torquay in 1871.

Jasper Bolton was only twenty-one when he took over the agency at Ballykisteen. He occupied the post until 1871 when the new Earl sold his property in Tipperary, and Ballykisteen passed into other hands. Jasper Bolton was then a sick man. He had moved to Limerick in September 1871 and he died there on 19 November. The circumstances of his death are described in a book written about him by his wife Emily. It is entitled *Quickly Ripened or Recollections of the late Jasper Bolton*. It was published privately and is undated. To quote the relevant paragraph:

"Early in 1869, on the occasion of an agrarian outrage in Tipperary, Jasper Bolton had, in the fulfilment of his duties as a magistrate, remained out all night in search of the offender, and was seized shortly afterwards with inflammation of the lungs, which, despite all that love and care could do, resulted in a slow but sure decline that finally terminated his earthly course at the early age of thirty years."

Emily Bolton's book *Quickly Ripened* about her husband dealt almost entirely with Jasper Bolton's religous life in the years immediately preceding his death. In her *Recollections* of her life at Dilston, written much later, she described her own religious experience which she linked up with an incident in her husband's life. She wrote that "as a child, she had been much influenced by a much-treasured book, 'Sermons for Children', into realizing that God was not a dread force but a way of salvation and a loving Father. These impressions remained with her in later years and after years of indifference and groping for something fuller and better, God's way of salvation was revealed to her when she was staying at Kilkee, County Clare." In her book about Jasper Bolton she described a religious experience in the seaside village of Kilkee in 1869 which she shared with her husband when he joined her at Kilkee shortly afterwards. After this he began to conduct weekly prayer-meetings at Ballykisteen. He had been a member of the Church of Ireland but withdrew in 1870 as he had felt unable to remain connected with any sect or church.

The portrait of Jasper Bolton reproduced in the book about him, shows him to have been a man of distinction. After his death he was described by an intimate friend in these words: "I was always struck by the great dignity and repose of his manner; also his purity of thought and expression."

In the spacious house of Ballykisteen there were altogether eight children, five Boltons and three De Pledges. Emily Bolton recorded that Jasper had treated the De Pledge children as if they were his own. Some years elapsed before Emily Bolton married F.W. Thomas, a widower who had a grown-up daughter. Mr. Thomas does not appear to have been a man of means and it has always been a puzzle to the author to know how Emily was able to educate her children. It should be noted that the eldest Bolton child, christened Edith Rhoda but known as Rhoda, married her cousin, Stanley Butler, second son of Josephine Butler, and that their son, Andrew Butler, was the author of *Portrait of Josephine Butler*, to which reference has been made.

## CONTEMPORARY HEALTH HAZARDS.

Two noteworthy features in the married lives of the six sisters are the number of children who died young and the longevity of the mothers. These features might appear to be incongruous but the explanation is that the deaths among the children occurred in the first half of the last century when medical standards were low, whereas the parents spent the greater part of their lives in the second half of the century when medical science was more advanced.

### Infant Mortality in the Family.

Reference has been made to a number of deaths among young people in the Grey family. Hannah, John Grey's elder sister, died at the age of five. One of his own children, a baby daughter, died in 1834. Three of the children of John Grey's eldest son, George Annett, died at a very early age as a result, respectively, of a fall, whooping-cough and measles. John Grey's youngest son, Charles, lost two of the three children by his wife, Emily Mary, probably from inflammation of the lungs. She herself died young, probably from the same illness.

At first sight this would appear to be

an unusually high mortality rate but account has to be taken of the size of these Victorian families with their large number of children, and also of the level of medical science.

Prevailing Standards of Medical Science.

The conclusion arrived at in a very recent study of the Victorian social system, entitled *Anne Thackeray Ritchie*, by Winifred Gerin, is that medical science in mid-Victorian days was dismally low and unable to prevent suffering even by the population who could pay high fees. The number of deaths of women in childbirth and of children chronicled in the record of a small group was described as appalling. This might be an over-statement where Northumberland was concerned but the following facts are indisputable. Smallpox had ceased to be a scourge with the discovery of vaccination in 1798 but there were occasional outbreaks of cholera. There was one in Gateshead in 1831 and also one in London in 1833. Sanitation and hygiene were deficient and disinfectants did not become effective until the 1870s. The great stride forward in surgery resulting from the replacement of ether by chloroform did not take place until 1847. Nursery routine was, in some respects, not conducive to the good health of children. Thus there were no bathrooms, baths being taken in tubs filled with hot or cold water, and there was a bias in favour of cold water for young children. At the same time nursery windows were kept closed by day and night.

Although midwifery was a time-honoured skill and there is no reason to suppose that in Northumberland it was below the prevailing standard, two of the Grey family died in childbirth or as a result of it: Elizabeth, wife of George Annett Grey and Maria, wife of George Butler, the son of Josephine and the Reverend George Butler.

Longevity of the Six Girls.

The longevity of the six sisters was remarkable and, in three cases, somewhat surprising. Eliza, Mrs. Masson, whose first husband died at an early age, was over eighty when she died. Tully, Mrs. Garston, survived her husband. She died in the middle of the 1880s when she was in her middle sixties. Fanny, Mrs. Smyttan, who was delicate as a child, survived her husband and died in 1895 aged seventy-two. Josephine, Mrs. Butler, who was not robust, died in 1906 aged seventy-eight, eight years after her husband. Harriet Meuricoffre died in 1900, or 1901, at the age of seventy. Emily Thomas was delicate as a child yet she survived all three husbands and died in 1922 aged eighty-six. She was a woman of great tenacity.

It is difficult to account for the longevity of the sisters. Their father was endowed with an exceptionally fine physique, and enjoyed very good health in his mature years and it may be that some of his physical characteristics had been transmitted to all six daughters. They had moreover spent their childhood in a well-ordered home and in healthy surroundings and were well-equipped to face the responsibilities inherent in family life.

# CHAPTER VIII

## THE GIRLS' POLITICAL AND RELIGIOUS LEANINGS

John Grey's daughters, with the exception of the youngest, were born during the period when he was actively engaged in local politics as an enthusiastic supporter of the Whig Party in its programme of social and economic measures disputed by the Tory Party.

On being appointed Receiver he withdrew from party politics but maintained his belief in the principles advocated by the Whigs. To quote from Josephine Butler's *Memoir* of him (p. 152), he scrupulously observed the condition that he should abstain from taking any active part in politics; "Nevertheless, he continued to take the keenest interest in public events and watched every sign of the progress of the principles which he believed to be sound".

John Grey maintained correspondence with members of the Whig Government of the day who were promoting measures of which he approved, such as the Repeal of the Corn Laws in 1846. When communicating with his daughters, after they had left home, he used to keep them informed of the political situation as he saw it. Thus he wrote to Mary Ann, wife of Edgar Garston, on 3 February 1864:

"I have been much interested in reading last night, *in extenso*,

Bright's speech at Birmingham in which he goes through with praise the great measures to which good old Lord Grey devoted all his political life. He not only lauds, as great measures, the justice of Catholic Emancipation, the Abolition of Tests, the Reform but above all the courage and statesmanship which overturned the old Poor Law ..... but he makes no reference to the Party to whom all this is owing. I well remember a private conversation with old Lord Grey, after retiring from public life, in which, talking of those subjects, he said that he thought it likely that the change of the Poor Law would reflect the greatest credit upon his Ministry hereafter of any of the measures which he had been instrumental in carrying. It had not been attended with the excitement of the Reform Bill or the splendour of the Abolition of Slavery, but it had checked the downward progress of the spirit of independence and manly bearing of the population of the country."

Their Political Leanings.

All six Grey girls unquestionably absorbed liberal principles from their father, and their mother's upbringing by parents who belonged to a church with a missionary tradition led to her influencing her children in a liberal direction, in the broad sense unconnected with party politics. There is no evidence that any of the daughters engaged actively in party politics in their own lifetime. Josephine Butler looked for support for her campaign for the abolition of the Contagious Diseases Acts where she could find it.

Support for the Whig Party at this period did not necessarily imply dislike of the Monarchy. Certainly the political bias of the Grey family in favour of the Whigs did not carry with it any anti-Royalist sentiments; rather the reverse. The Grey family were traditionally staunch patriots as a result of their border ancestry and their patriotism carried with it a devotion to the sovereign, although not necessarily to the incumbent of the throne. In England the Royal family had lost the respect of the people earlier in the century on account of the treatment of Queen Caroline by King George IV. A Whig named Brougham was mainly responsible for King George abandoning his attempt to divorce her in 1821. He subsequently became Lord Chancellor in a Whig Government in 1832. That the Grey family had no bias against Queen Victoria on accession is clear from an exuberant letter written by Margaretta Grey to her brother in July 1837: "How exquisite is the weather. Everything so beautiful and promising for the country, and the political world all alive and full of expectation under the auspices of our youthful sovereign".

The support which Queen Victoria derived from the Whigs in 1839 enabled her to retain the sympathy of the Whig families such as the Greys. Queen Victoria began to make an appeal to the middle-classes when she and Prince Albert embarked on a staid family life revolving round their children. The popular interest in the comings and goings of the Royal family was illustrated by Emily Grey's description of the excitement of the people of Alnwick on the occasion of the Royal party entraining at Little Mills Station in 1850. By the time of the Great Exhibition in 1851, which year saw the defeat of the Whigs, Queen Victoria and Prince Albert had won a place in the hearts of the people on their own merits and without regard to party politics.

Their Religious Leanings.
The six Grey sisters were greatly influenced by the religious views of their parents which were strikingly similar although their backgrounds were different. Both were Protestants and both attached more importance to the congregation than to church hierarchy. John Grey went to an Anglican school whereas Hannah was educated at a Moravian boarding-school, as was noted earlier. Both had a leaning towards evangelicalism with its emphasis on belief in the redemption of mankind. John Grey might be described as a Low Church Anglican. He much admired John Wesley

(1703–1791), the founder of the evangelical Methodist movement, and he built a small chapel for the Methodists in the neighbourhood of Dilston, although he himself attended Corbridge Parish Church. John Wesley himself was for a time greatly attracted by the Moravian Church.

Mary Ann Garston was a regular worshipper in Aigburth Parish Church over many years. Josephine and Emily had leanings towards Nonconformism. Josephine Butler drew much of her support from Quakers and Emily numbered Quakers among her close friends; these included the Bragg family which was connected with Newcastle and Plymouth. Two Bragg sisters, old friends of hers, had inspired her to set down the *Recollections* of her childhood. Hatty Meuricoffre and her husband were strong supporters of the Protestant community in Naples.

St. Andrew's Church, Corbridge was a focal point for the Grey sisters from their youth up and all were married there. The church contains three stained-glass windows set in the East wall. Across the base of the windows is written: To the glory of God and in loving remembrance of Hannah Eliza wife of John Grey Esq. Dilston who entered into rest on the Eve of the Ascension, May 16th 1860, aged sixty-six years, by her daughters and granddaughters.

Efforts made by the author to ascertain when these windows were installed have been unavailing. The probability is that this was during the lifetime of John Grey, who died in 1868. Had the windows been installed after this date, one would have expected them to be in his memory also seeing that both he and Hannah were buried in the churchyard of St. Andrew's, as their adjoining tombs testify.

The proximity of views then maintaining between Anglicans, Moravians, and Methodists, is today being manifested in the proposed convenant between the Church of England, the Methodist Church, the Moravian Church, the United Reform Church and the Churches of Christ. The proposed convenant has received provisional approval from the General Synod of the Church of England and is now being considered by Dioceses.

# CHAPTER IX

## EPILOGUE

Biographies soon out of Print.

In the Introduction reference was made to *Early Victorian England 1830-65*, edited by G.M. Young, OUP 1934, Third Impression 1963. Attention was drawn to the fact that no reference was made to Josephine Butler although two contemporaries, Elizabeth Fry and Florence Nightingale, were mentioned.

It must be born in mind that *Early Victorian England* was first published nearly fifty years ago and that interest in Josephine Butler has waxed and waned. In the latter half of the nineteenth century interest in her work as a social reformer declined once her campaign had come to a successful conclusion. There was a revival of interest in the first part of the century, in anticipation of her centenary 1828–1928, but it too was not sustained for long. A primary reason for the decline in interest in Josephine Butler in the last century was that the numerous writings by her had only a limited output, were soon out of print and were not republished. This fact also explains the lack of knowledge of the achievements of John Grey in Northumberland.

At first the only publicity that his work achieved was in Josephine Butler's *Memoir of John Grey of Dilston*, which was first published in 1869, the year after his death, with a revised edition in 1875. In the *Memoir* John Grey was seen through the eyes of a daughter who described her father's life as a whole, although Josephine did in fact devote one of the ten chapters of her book, (Chapter VIII pp 213-247), to his achievements as an agriculturist, which she described in a very professional manner. The chapter emphasises that John Grey acquired an international reputation on account of his advocacy of scientific methods: the use of chemical fertilizers, improved drainage methods, modern agricultural machinery, long leases, limitation of game preservation. His writings and speeches were read in France, Germany, Holland and Sweden. He was consulted by the Emperor of Austria and the Minister of Public Works in Sweden. When he resided at Dilston Hall visits were paid by Swedes, Russians and French seeking his advice. They were accommodated and hospitably entertained. A frequent visitor was Baron Justus von Liebig (1803-1873). He was a pioneer in agricultural chemistry, especially artificial manures, and he discovered a process for manufacturing meat extracts.

As the *Memoir of John Grey* was never republished, appreciation of his achievements was at first restricted to the relatively few who had access to the book. An author who appreciated the stature of John Grey as an agriculturist was Richard Wilford. His book *Men of*

*Mark Twixt Tyne and Tweed*, 1895, which was noted earlier, was about Northumberland. It contained a chapter on John Grey. Richard Wilford concluded by saying that Josephine Butler's *Memoir of John Grey* was a delightful book which every true Northumbrian read with pride and pleasure. Mr. Grey would always be remembered as a benefactor to the British farmer. The better part of his life was spent in the endeavour to increase and multiply the fruits of the earth. He was a striking type of that robust race of Englishman of which the north-eastern district had been prolific.

Since 1890 John Grey's name has figured in a good article of a column and a half in the *Dictionary of National Biography*.

Today, writers who glean pieces of information about him from books which are primarily about Josephine Butler are liable inadvertently to misrepresent his stature as an agriculturist. To take an example. In a comparatively recent book about Liverpool College, entitled *Liverpool Gentlemen*, Faber & Faber 1960, the author, David Wainright, touched on the parentage of Josephine Butler. In the course of describing very fully and well the place of her husband, the Rev. George Butler, in the history of the College, the author made a brief reference to John Grey (p.118). It shows that he had not availed himself of material such as the article in *The Dictionary of National Biography*, Vol. 8

(1921), correctly to describe the status of John Grey as an agriculturist. There is also an unfortunate error in names. Referring to the marriage of the Rev. George Butler, the author wrote:

> "But he had met and married Josephine Grey. Her father was John Grey of Dilston, a Northumberland farmer, who was an authority on both 'beasts' and 'crops'; her mother, the extraordinary Margaretta Grey of Edinburgh, who as a girl, dressed in boy's clothes and penetrated to the Gallery of the House of Commons and listened to a debate".

Mr. Wainwright was wrong in stating that Josephine's mother was Margaretta Grey. Her mother was Hannah Eliza, daughter of Ralph Annett of Alnwick. Margaretta Grey, the lady to whom he refers, was a sister of John Grey who married her cousin, the Rev. Henry Grey, Doctor of Divinity in the Church of Scotland. The epithet "extraordinary" is not applicable either to John Grey's wife or to his sister, Margaretta, who was a woman with a fine intellect and advanced views about the education and status of women.

Two Standard Works Compared.

The two standard works of recent years on Josephine Butler are undoubtedly *Portrait of Josephine Butler* by A.S.G. Butler, 1954 and *Josephine Butler - Flame*

*of Fire* by E. Moberly Bell, 1962. A.S.G.
Butler depicted his grandmother as he
knew her from his youth up until he was
eighteen. He described her campaign as
he saw it after studying her personal
letters, which numbered nearly a
thousand, and books by and about her.
Miss Bell undertook her book with the
encouragement of the Butler Society
which, to quote from her Author's Note,
felt the need of an authoritative
biography of Josephine Butler that could
be put into the hands of the present
generation. She had access to the mass
of Josephine's correspondence housed in
various libraries.

Miss Bell described her book as a
biography but it is essentially a history
of Josephine Butler's work as a social
reformer, of the campaign which she
waged throughout her life for the
betterment of the status of women. Miss
Bell touched only lightly on family
matters and, in so doing, dealt with
certain subjects with which she was not
well-acquainted. Not surprisingly, her
references to John Grey and members of
his family contain some inaccuracies
which need to be corrected in order that
they should not be perpetuated.

In connection with the appointment of
John Grey as Receiver of the Greenwich
Hospital Estates in Northumberland, Miss
Bell wrote (p.19): "He abundantly
justified the choice. In the forty years
in which he administered the estates
their value and their revenue vastly

increased". In fact, as was pointed out in the Introduction to this study, John Grey's working life covered exactly sixty years, of which thirty years, from 1833 to 1863, were in the capacity of Receiver. Miss Bell failed to draw a clear distinction between the first period of thirty years when John Grey was a landed proprietor and tenant farmer deeply involved in local politics, and the subsequent period of thirty years during which he filled the post of administrator of the Greenwich Hospital Estates and was required, by the terms of his employment, to keep aloof from party politics.

There are three other minor errors. Firstly, Margaretta Grey was described (p.16) as the younger of John Grey's two sisters whereas she was the elder and much the more forceful. Secondly, Miss Bell wrote (p.23) that Eliza, the eldest of the six Grey sisters, had married a business man who worked in China, whence she wrote letters which were eagerly read. In fact, Eliza's husband was a distinguished surgeon, William Morrison, F.R.C.S., who died in Hong Kong in 1853. The description "business man" would appropriately describe Mary Ann's husband, William Garston, in his mature years, although in his youth he was an adventurer, a Philhellene, who fought on the side of the Greeks in the Greek War of Independence. Thirdly, when the Grey family moved to Dilston in 1835, there were not nine children, as stated by Miss Bell, but only eight – three sons and five daughters – taking into account that a baby girl, Ellie, had died in infancy in 1834 and that the youngest of the six sisters, Emily, was born in Dilston House itself in 1836.

## Josephine Butler's Religious Outlook.

A.S.G. Butler and Miss Bell covered a considerable amount of common ground and it is surprising that Miss Bell's book, which followed that of Andrew Butler by eight years, contains only a single reference to his book in both text and Index, and that a quite unimportant one about a quotation. At the same time Miss Bell drew extensively on Mr. Butler's book for details of Josephine's upbringing and family. A possible explanation is that the approach of the two authors was markedly different when dealing with the complicated question of Josephine Butler's religious beliefs. Miss Bell was much more concerned with her campaigning activities than with her mental processes. She dealt briefly with the mysticism in Josephine Butler's religious outlook, comparing her with Catharine of Siena, about whom Josephine had written a book. Miss Bell wrote: "Like Josephine herself Catharine was conscious of a direct call to costly service. In Catharine's mystical experience we can trace Josephine's. We have one mystic portrayed by another".

A.S.G. Butler, for his part, described someone he knew intimately as he saw her. He devoted a whole chapter entitled "The Instrument of Prayer", to describing Josephine's religious life, with special emphasis on her conviction that prayer could be used as an instrument. He identified two aspects of her faith: her delight in the Saints, and her interest and belief in the spiritual healing of bodily ailments.

He pointed out that she was drawn to the Saints and Martyrs because they were witnesses to Divine Truth through the ages and taught men the love of God. They did not shrink from challenging evil-doers. Saint Catharine was a mystic because she belonged to a sect which professed to have direct intercourse with God. Josephine was a mystic because she had the gift of communion with God.

A.S.G. Butler considered that Josephine's intense religious faith was a gift, the ability to commune with God through prayer; especially intercessory prayer for others, to the extent of applying her physical suffering vicariously for others. Intercessory prayer was a preoccupation; so many people wrote to her for help.

For the information of readers who may be wondering what is meant by a mystic, a scientific study of Mysticism was undertaken by the late Dean Inge, Dean of St. Paul's Cathedral. He defined a mystic as follows: "The mystic has a clear vision of eternal ideas and can apprehend the unity that lies behind them".

Spiritual Healing of Body Ailments.

This is how A.S.G. Butler described Josephine Butler's interest and belief in the spiritual healing of bodily ailments. She saw no reason why people should not be miraculously cured as a result of prayer. He quoted her as saying "there is not a word in the whole Bible which intimated that the beautiful and beneficient gifts of healing were to cease at a given date or forever". In 1886 she recorded the case of M. Henri Laserres, a distinguished French political writer and a professed free-thinker. An infection of the eyes threatened his sight. No oculist could arrest the trouble so he went to Lourdes and was completely cured. That occurred in 1874 and on his return M. Laserres discovered a copy of the Gospels in Latin, was amazed at their contents, and spent the next ten years translating them into admirable French.

"At about the same time in her life", A.S.G. Butler wrote, "my grandmother, too, was much impressed by an institute called the House of Healing in North London; it must have been a quite sincere undertaking because that level-headed man, George Butler, said 'I wish some of the Church theologians, like Canon Westcott, would go and see for themselves and write about it, and not stand aside and ignore such wonders'."

Revival of Interest in Josephine Butler.

The omission today of any reference to Josephine Butler from a work similar to *Early Victorian England 1830-65* would be unlikely, bearing in mind the revival of interest in her, especially in Germany and the United States, not only as a social reformer but as an advocate of education for women and a feminist.

It is noteworthy that Josephine Butler was included in *The Oxford Dictionary of the Christian Church*, edited by F.L. Cross, first published in 1957 and republished in 1958. The item reads as follows:

BUTLER, Josephine Elizabeth (1828-1906) social reformer. She was the daughter of John Grey of Dilston and in 1852 married George Butler (1819-90) sometime Canon of Winchester. Her main interest was the reclamation of prostitutes and the suppression of the 'white slave trade'. To this end she formed in 1869 the Ladies' National Association for the Repeal of the Contagious Diseases Acts, and in 1875 called a meeting at Geneva which resulted in the establishment of the International Federation for the Abolition of the State Regulation of Vice. Her inspiring work can best be studied in her *Personal Reminiscences of a Great Crusade* (in 1896). Behind her activities as a reformer lay a life of almost continuous prayer in which she took as her model St. Catharine of Siena (whose life she published in 1878).

The inclusion of her name in the *Alternative Service Book 1980*, on the decision of the Synod of the Church of England, is likely to help in keeping her memory green for a while.


The Phenomenal Recovery of Thomas Bolton.

Certain events involving the Bolton family have a strange relevance to the interest and belief of Josephine Butler in the spiritual healing of bodily ailments. They are therefore included at the close of this work.

The family of Jasper Bolton and his wife Emily consisted of two boys and three girls. The eldest son, Thomas (born 1 December 1863) was very delicate. He migrated to Australia in 1885, when aged twenty-one. The author's father, Arthur Bolton, who was four years younger than Thomas, died in 1912 of inflammation of the lungs. In 1913 my mother married a regular soldier, Edward Rogers. The War of 1914-18 intervened. Major Rogers, R.E., M.C., was killed in the Battle of the Somme, (dying of wounds on 8 December, 1916), and family contacts were gravely disrupted for a number of years.

Thomas Bolton married a Miss Emma Charlotte Tysh of Launceston, Tasmania and had five children by her: Adelaise,

Jasper, Geoffrey, Corina and John. In 1917 the author was visited at school in England by two stalwart sons of Thomas Bolton, Jasper and Geoffrey, who were then in the Australian Forces.

In 1928 Jasper Bolton wrote from Australia to say that his father, Thomas Bolton, had died on 1 August, 1928 aged sixty-four. He commented: "It is remarkable to think that Father was carried off the boat to die at Port Adelaide many years ago on arrival here from England, and he has only just now gone".

Veronica Rogers*, my half-sister, had, after her mother's death, made her career in Australia as a plant breeder. In the spring of 1972, when in Australia, I accompanied my sister to an apiarist, Mr. G. Loft of Echuca, Victoria, whose advice she was seeking in connection with her work. My attention was attracted by a wooden frame such as is used in a bee-hive, which was boldly marked T.B. This led to my learning that Thomas Bolton had started up as a bee-keeper at Portland in the State of Victoria in 1886. In this capacity he achieved a State-wide reputation. He was the first President of the Victorian Apiarist Association and published many articles on frame-hives. A hive devised by him was named after him. This hive of several storeys allowed the interchange of frames. A firm, Pender Bros. Ltd., manufacturers of West Maitland, NSW. manufactured and sold The Modified

*Now Mrs Gordon McK. Henry, M.B.E.

Bolton Hive comprising eight storeys. A contemporary advertisement by Pender Bros. Ltd., describes The Modified Bolton Hive and System in minute detail.

Thomas Bolton's daughter, Adelaise, married an Englishman, R.G. Weeks who had been convalescing in her father's care at Lambrook, a homestead in Victoria. Adelaise and her husband had three sons, two of whom served in the Pacific in the 1939–45 War. After the War, both went into Christian Service; one with aborigines and the other in Youth Evangelism. After her husband's death, Adelaise Weeks, who shared her father's religious beliefs, became an Evangelist. A short biography of her was published in 1966. She died on 6 December 1971 aged seventy-five.

In 1972, when going through some letters from Josephine Butler which were left me by her grandson, Andrew Butler, I came across a photo-copy of a letter dated 26 March 1884 from Josephine to her son Stanley. An extract from this letter is reproduced below. The "George" referred to in it was Josephine's eldest son.

"George stays in London next Sunday to look after Arthur Bolton who is coming up to try for examination – for a naval engineer. I hope he may succeed, poor boy. He will stay with George. Tom Bolton, who is very ill, is coming with him, to go to the House of

Healing in North London. If he is not healed bodily, he will, I am sure, come back with a new light and joy. I must tell you sometime of the day I spent there. Father, who is interested in it, says he wishes some of the Church theologians, like Canon Westcott, would go and see for themselves, and write about it, and not stand aside and ignore such great blessings and wonders as God is working for us now on Earth. There is not a word in the whole Bible which intimates that the beautiful and beneficent gifts of healing were to cease at a given date and forever. But the contrary evidence may be found. Many doctors now go to see the work and are convinced."

I was not aware of Thomas Bolton's visit at the age of twenty to the House of Healing until after I had learnt about his long and full life, the shaping of which would seem to endorse Josephine Butler's belief in the spiritual healing of bodily ailments.

# BIBLIOGRAPHY

Arnold, Ralph. The Unhappy Countess and her grandson John Bowes. (Constable 1957)

Arnold, Ralph. Northern Lights. The Story of Lord Derwentwater. (Constable 1959)

Bell, E. Moberly. Josephine Butler. Flame of Fire. (Constable 1962)

Bolton, Emily. Quickly Ripened or Recollections of the late Jasper Bolton. (John F. Shaw undated)

Butler, A.S.G. Portrait of Josephine Butler. (Faber & Faber 1954)

Butler, Josephine E. Memoir of John Grey of Dilston. (H.S. King, Revised edition 1875)

Butler, Josephine E. In Memoriam Harriet Meuricoffre. (Horace Marshall 1901)

Fawcett M.G. & Turner, E.M. 'osephine Butler. (The Association for Moral & Social Hygiene 1927)

Garston, Edgar. Greece Revisited & Sketches in Lower Egypt in 1840 with Thirty-six Hours of a Campaign in Greece in 1825. An Extract from my Journal (Saunders & Otley 1842)

Hepple, Edmund. Milfield MS. Genealogy of the Grey Family of Northumberland. (Metchim & Burt 1856)

Hogarth, D.G. & others. The Balkans, (Clarendon Press, Oxford 1915)

Johnson, George W. & Lucy, A. Josephine E. Butler, An Autobiographical Memoir, (Arrowsmith 1909)

116

St.Clair, William L.    That Greece might
        Still be Free. The Philhellenes in
        the War of Independence. (O.U.P.
        1972)
Wainright, David.    Liverpool Gentlemen.
        A    History    of    Liverpool    College.
        (Faber & Faber 1960)

# INDEX

## A

## B

Braemar Gathering. 37.
Bragg family. 100.
Brougham, H.P., 98.
Budd, Mrs. Ethel. 66.
Butler, Arthur Stanley. 73, 75, 91, 114.
Butler, (Andrew) A.S.G. 1, 14, 18, 27,
     40, 76, 78, 91, 106, 108, 109.
Butler, George Grey. 73, 75.
Butler, Rev. George. 27, 40, 66, 69,
     72-75, 104, 111.
Butler, Josephine. 1, 6, 14, 21, 30, 40-
     44, 66-79, 94-100, 102-115.
Butler, Rhoda. 1, 76, 89, 91.
Burn, John. 6.
Burn, Mary. 6.
Byron, Lord. 56.

C

Carlisle. 20, 29.
Caroline, Queen. 32, 98.
Caserta. 82.
Catharine of Siena, St. 108.
Charlotte, Queen. 9.
Charlton Hall, Ellingham. 67.
Cheltenham College. 74.
Chester. 56, 64.
China. 33, 107.
Church House, Westminster. 67.
Church of England, Synod of. 79, 101,
                 112.
Cobbett, William. 32.
Cook, Thomas. 30, 85.
Corbridge. 13, 15, 29.
Corbridge, St. Andrew's Church. 24, 42,
     49, 67, 72, 80, 100.
Corn Laws, (1836). 96.

Corpus Christi, Cambridge. 67, 71.
Coquetdale Ward. 20.
Crimean War. 25.
Crockford's Clerical Directory. 68.
Cross, F.L. 111.
Cullen, County Tipperary. 88, 89.
Culley, George. 10.
Custozza, Battle of. 84.

## D

Darling, Grace. 35, 36.
De Pledge, William. 87, 91.
Derby, Lord. 88, 89.
Derwentwater, Earl of. 13.
Devil's Water. 13, 15.
Dictionary of National Biography. 104.
Dilston Hall. 14–20, 29, 35, 42, 80, 86, 103.
Dilston House. 15, 16, 18, 107.
Durham. 20, 49, 67.
Durham, Lord. 11.
Durham University. 19, 72, 75.

## E

Early Victorian England. 3, 111.
Edinburgh. 9, 30, 33, 37.
Egypt. 85.
Ellingham-with-Alnwick. 67.
Erard, Sebastien. 40.
Eugenie, Empress. 38.
Exeter College, Oxford. 73.
Exhibition, Great 1851. 38, 99.

# F

Fanny Grey (See Grey, Frances)
Farne Islands. 36.
Flint House School. 9.
Forfarshire S.S. 36.
France, Emperor of. 52.
Fry, Elizabeth. 4, 102.
Fulneck Girls School. 23.
Fulneck Boys School, Pudsey. 23.

# G

Garibaldi. 82,
Garston, Edgar.55-66, 107.
Garston, Gwendoline, Miss. 66.
Garston, Mary Ann. 55, 64-66, 94, 100.
Gateshead. 87, 93.
Gladstone, William Ewart. 76.
Glendale Ward. 4, 6, 77.
George IV, King. 32, 98.
Greece. 58-64.
Greek War of Independence. 55-64, 107.
Greenwich Hospital Estates. 2, 12-16, 43, 89, 106.
Grey, Charles. 19, 38, 40, 88-89, 92.
Grey, Col. Charles. 35.
Grey, Earl. 8, 12, 13.
Grey, Eliza. (see Morrison) 14, 49.
Grey, Emily. (see Bolton) 14-15, 18, 26, 31, 34-39, 41, 50.
Grey, Frances. (see Smyttan) 16, 18, 21, 27, 36, 41.
Grey, George (Father of J.G.). 6.
Grey, George Annett (Son of J.G.). 14, 26, 37, 92, 94.
Grey, Hannah. 6, 10, 14, 17, 22, 26, 41, 99, 105.

Kilkee, County Clare. 91.
Kirknewton. 77.

## L

Lablache, Luigi. 39.
Laserres, Henri. 110.
Latrobe, Benjamin. 23.
Latrobe, Christian Ignatius. 23.
Leupold, Edith. 54, 69.
Leupold, Marie. 54.
Liebig, Baron Eustace. 103.
Linnaeus, Carolus. 26.
Linnaean Society. 26.
Lipwood House. 42, 69.
Liverpool. 55, 66, 69.
Liverpool College. 66, 74, 75, 104.
Liverpool Collegiate Institution. 74.
London. 9, 30. 93.

## M

Masson, Mrs. 54, 86, 94.
Melbourne, Lord. 12.
Mendelssohn. 39.
Methodists. 100, 101.
Meuricoffre, Harriet. 70, 79–86, 94, 100.
Meuricoffre, Sophie. 84.
Meuricoffre, Tell. 80, 82, 85.
Meuricoffre, Thekla. 85.
Milan. 84.
Milfield Hill. 9, 10, 14, 20, 26, 33, 45, 49, 55, 77.
Missolonghi. 56.
Moravian Church. 23, 101.
Moravian School, (see Fulneck) 22, 99.
Morpeth. 4, 6, 36.

## Q

Quakers. 87, 100.

## R

Radcliffe, Charles. 13.
Radcliffe family. 12.
Red Shirt Volunteers. 82.
Reform Bill.(1832) 12.
Richmond School. 7-8.
Rogers, Major Edward. 112.
Rogers, Veronica. 113.
Rothbury. 20.
Royal College of Surgeons. 50.

## S

Sadowa, Battle of. 84.
Sidney Sussex College, Cambridge. 8.
Sinclair, Sir John. 11.
Smyttan, Frances. 67-71, 94.
Smyttan, Rev. G.H. 67-68, 70-71.
St. Andrew's University. 75.
St. Clair, W.L. 56, 63, 64.
Stephenson, George. 30.
Stephenson, Robert. 30.
Sterndale Bennett. 40.
Suliotes. 58.
Switzerland. 76-77, 83, 85-86.

## T

Tate, James. 7.
Tipperary. 90.
Thomas, Emily. 34, 91, 94.
Thomas, F.W. 91.

Tidy, Miss. 19.
Turkey. 56, 61, 64.
Tynedale District Council. 45.

V

Venice. 84.
Vestris, Mme. 39.
Vesuvius, Eruption of. 84.
Victor Emmanuel, King. 82.
Victoria, Queen. 4, 25, 37, 40, 49, 98.
Victorian Era. 2.

W

Wainwright, David. 75, 105.
Wards, Administrative. 4.
Weeks, Adelaise. 114.
Weeks, R.G. 114.
Wesley, John. 99, 100.
Whig Party. 11, 96–98.
Wilford, Richard. 44, 103.
William IV, King. 12.
Winchester Cathedral. 76.
Wooler. 77.

Y

Young, Arthur. 11.